SELECTING AND DEVELOPING MEDIA FOR INSTRUCTION

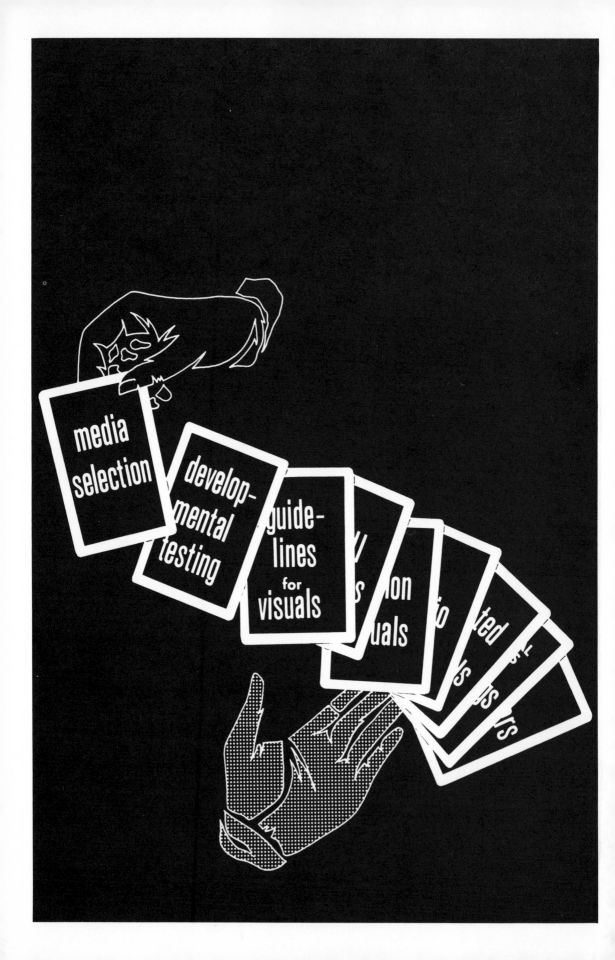

SELECTING AND DEVELOPING MEDIA FOR INSTRUCTION

Ronald H. Anderson

Bell System Center for Technical Education

With Illustrations by Pat Lynch

American Society for Training and Development
Madison, Wisconsin

VAN NOSTRAND REINHOLD COMPANY

NEW YORK   CINCINNATI   ATLANTA   DALLAS   SAN FRANCISCO
LONDON   TORONTO   MELBOURNE

Van Nostrand Reinhold Company Regional Offices:
New York   Cincinnati   Atlanta   Dallas   San Francisco

Van Nostrand Reinhold Company International Offices:
London   Toronto   Melbourne

Library of Congress Catalog Card Number: 76-18745
ISBN: 0-442-20350-0

Manufactured in the United States of America

Published by Van Nostrand Reinhold Company
450 West 33rd Street, New York, N.Y. 10001
and
American Society for Training and Development
P.O. Box 5307, Madison, Wisconsin 53705

Published simultaneously in Canada by Van Nostrand Reinhold Ltd.

15 14 13 12 11 10 9 8 7 6 5 4 3 2

Library of Congress Cataloging in Publication Data

Anderson, Ronald H.
    Selecting and developing media for instruction.

    Bibliography: p.
    Includes index.
    1. Educational technology.   I. Title.
LB1028.3.A5   371.3'078   76-18745
ISBN 0-442-20350-0

Foreword

We live in a world of media. Our nation's young people are called the "Television Generation," because most of them spend more hours in front of the TV than they do in school. We are a visual culture, living in an environment impacted by media messages of every kind. And through experience, we've grown increasingly sophisticated in the way we both witness and contribute to the communication envelope which surrounds us.

Because of our unique mass orientation to electronic and visual media, and our advanced skills in their utilization, it is not surprising that the United States is acknowledged worldwide as the undisputed leader in communications technology.

In recent years, we've also seen media assume an increasingly important role in every aspect of instructional planning and design. The process began with the use of "visual aids" in support of instructor-centered teaching ... evolving until today, when we frequently see audio-visual and audio-video media assigned center-stage prominence, especially for student individualized self-instruction and remote access individualized instruction.

And as the media and our audience have grown more sophisticated, the challenge to develop effective skills in communications technology has grown in parallel scope and importance.

To develop these skills, the practitioner must begin with an understanding of the various media available—and how each might best be selected and utilized in an instructional environment. The process of such understanding and selection is the central theme of this book.

Up to this time, there has been only limited professional literature on the crucial subject of media evaluation and selection for teaching and training. Many authors have provided detailed descriptions of the *characteristics* of various audio-visual/video presentation systems; but when faced with the question of *which* to use *when*, most fall back to the empirical (but not very helpful) concept that the "best medium" is simply the "least expensive one that works."

This book starts from there, and offers a highly readable, highly logical discussion of a *system* to evaluate instructional media and identify the most appropriate choice to accomplish communications objectives. The book is designed to serve as a ready reference source to assist instructional planners and course writers in decision-making. The system described is practical and proof-tested, and can be extremely helpful for *any* media practitioner, regardless of field or level of experience.

We wish to thank our colleague and friend, Dr. Richard B. Lewis, who provided invaluable assistance in manuscript preparation, and the Media Division of ASTD which accepted responsibility for its publication.

P. Kevin O'Sullivan
Executive Vice President
American Society for Training and Development

Acknowledgments

As will be noted in the introduction, this book "is not the first word on the subject [of media and instruction], for without the diligent work of many people this book could not have been written." For their contributions to this field, I am most grateful. This will certainly not be the last word on the subject either, for only through the efforts of future researchers and writers can this relatively young field be advanced. We

...only the tip of the iceberg.

...ke to the field of media and learn-
...ne very nice people. I wish to ex-
...RUDY BRETZ, JERRY KEMP, SUE
...r time, patience, and encourage-
...wis for his kind words and many
...order of my chaotic manuscripts;
...ience and understanding through-

R. A.

About the Author . . .

Ronald H. Anderson is an Instructional Technologist in the Bell System Center for Technical Education in Lisle, Illinois. Among his responsibilities are research into learning, and the training of course developers to prepare lesson materials. Mr. Anderson is a member of numerous professional organizations, including the National Audio-Visual Association, Association for Educational Communications and Technology, and Illinois Training Directors Association. He also serves on the Media Division board of directors of the American Society for Training and Development, is a member of the Curriculum council and faculty for the NAVA—Indiana University Communications Seminars and has published articles in the IMPROVING HUMAN PERFORMANCE RESEARCH JOURNAL for the National Society for Performance and Instruction.

Contents

1 Introduction

This book is intended as a reference guide or job-aid for anyone involved with the process of selecting media and planning the development of media for instructional purposes. Although it is aimed primarily at course writers and instructors who are required to perform these tasks, it can also be a valuable tool for managers of training departments or supervisors of course development programs.

PROBLEMS OF MEDIA SELECTION

Selecting the best medium or media for instructional purposes is not an easy job, as anyone who has struggled with the problem can testify. The choice is complex and difficult because it is based upon a combination of interrelated factors, exemplified by these questions:

To what degree must the training imitate or simulate real working conditions and environments?

What medium or media would be most practical for packaging, implementing, and updating the program?

Is equipment needed to use the medium selected, and if so, is it readily available? Is special equipment justified to implement the course?

To what extent must student achievements after training be exactly according to prescription?

Does the value of the course—the amount of behavior change, the number of students to be trained, or the life of the course—justify the cost of the medium or media considered?

These questions, and many others that must be answered in the process of course development, indicate the complexity of the problem. Yet, they also suggest that selecting the media best able to assure student achievement of course objectives, is an integral part of the entire course planning process. The skillful course developer demonstrates ability to evaluate and balance priorities among the many choices available. He develops courses that not only meet student requirements, but at the same time respect organizational realities.

Unfortunately, there are few guidelines available to help a course developer to make decisions about media. There are no simple, foolproof formulas or reference tables that match any specific medium with any particular course objectives. Validated historical data or research reports about various media used for instruction in widely differing circumstances are spare, and what are available are often contradictory and imprecise.

OTHER RELATED PROBLEMS

The total cost of using each medium and its accompanying equipment is often difficult to determine. In addition, the rate of technological advances has caused equipment to become obsolete extremely fast. Literature extolling the virtues of various types of hardware is available, but is often misleading and unhelpful.

Recently, however, much progress has been made toward developing a solid basis for the development of instruction with media. The term widely used to represent this trend is *instructional technology*. The definition below, taken from a March 1970 report to the President and the Congress of the United States,[1] explains the term, and lays a basis for the purposes of this book:

In order to reflect present-day reality, the Commission has had to look at the pieces that make up instructional technology: television, films, overhead projectors, computers, and the other items of "hardware" and "software" (to use the convenient jargon that distinguishes machines from programs). In nearly every case, these media have entered education independently, and still operate more in isolation than in combination. . . . Instruc-

[1]Commission On Instructional Technology To Improve Learning, *A report to the President and the Congress of the United States* (Washington, D.C.: U.S. Government Printing Office, 1970), p. 19.

tional technology goes beyond any particular medium or device....It is a systematic way of designing, carrying out, and evaluating the total process of learning, teaching, and communication, and employing a combination of human and nonhuman resources to bring about more effective instruction.

An earlier study by the American Institutes for Research,[2] pointed out that there is no generally understood rationale as to why some information is presented by motion pictures rather than by programmed instruction in print or by textbooks rather than by slides and audio tape, for example. Often, the only apparent reason for a choice is the background of the production talent: film makers work in their medium and text writers work in theirs. Thus, competition among media producers, or the availability of a talent, has a strong influence on what training materials are produced. Such practices are encouraged by the absence of theory and procedural practices upon which media selection can be based.

The problem of media selection has been further complicated by a tendency for course developers to consider media selection as an isolated and independent function that is undertaken at some point well along in the instructional development process. This viewpoint has sometimes resulted from attempts to make the media selection process as scientific and exact as possible. Although the goal seems worthy, the present reality does not permit scientifically precise decisions. Thus, the process of instructional technology as a total system provides a means for consideration of all essential elements in course development—and at the appropriate time for each.

NECESSARY ASSUMPTIONS

Within the instructional technology process, however, there is continuing need for aids to making decisions about media—what to use, when, and why. This book is offered as a practical handbook in this important activity for all developers of training programs. It is not the first word on the subject, for without the diligent work of many people this book could not have been written. It certainly won't be the last word, either, but it sets forth a practical procedure to aid course developers in this process.

The content of this book is based on a number of assumptions that need to be accepted:

- Consider media selection as an integral part of the total instructional development process.

[2]American Institutes for Research Monograph 2, *Instructional Media: A Procedure for The Design of Multi-Media Instruction; A Critical Review Of Research and Suggestions For Future Research* (Pittsburgh: American Institute for Research, 1966).

- The selection of efficient and effective media for instruction requires balancing lesson content and purposes with the characteristics of specific media.[3]
- In the selection process, compromises are often made, and will of necessity be made. By using the procedures suggested here, however, decisions by whim, convenience, or political judgment, can perhaps be replaced by decisions based upon analysis and program design.

Finally, before we enter a discussion of how to use this book, you should know that there are at least three different circumstances for which it has been designed:

- For use as a minitext in a formal or informal course for instructional development personnel.
- As a self-instruction textbook to assist a new course developer to become acquainted with various media useful for training and education.
- As a job-aid, to be used as a reference in day-to-day course development, to assure attention to the relevant decisions that must be made in selecting and developing media.

This is not a textbook in media production, for many volumes would be required to treat the production of the many useful media in sufficient depth. However, the guidelines provided here will quickly give you sufficient background to work in the practical problem of media selection and development, and to determine what additional knowledge you need that can be obtained from such other sources as publications, workshops, and association with production personnel.

Before undertaking the media selection and development procedures, which are the principal content of this book, an example of the total instructional development process is presented below. Though a tongue-in-cheek spirit is maintained in the example, two principal points are emphasized: first, media are always selected in the context of a total instructional development process; and second, *even before we decide to train* we must be sure that a need for training exists.

A Case Example of the Instructional Development Process

Suppose the boss is tired of seeing wads of wastepaper scattered over the floors in the company offices, and he wants it stopped. Since the desks of employees are all ten feet from the wastebaskets, and since leav-

[3]R. H. Anderson, "Selection of Media: Another Perspective," *Improving Human Performance*, Vol. 3, No. 3 (Fall 1974), pp. 81–107.

ing a desk to dispose of a wad of paper is a loss of valuable time, the boss states that all employees must be trained to hit the baskets, and he wants a training film made right now! It seems logical that analysis of the situation would suggest that this is not really a training problem at all; someone should convince the boss that more wastebaskets, properly located, would save time and money, and reduce hazards from sailing wads. So, the implication is that in the consideration of training needs, often solutions are found for important problems that are *not* problems that should be solved by instruction.

The message is: try to eliminate unnecessary training. Search for the problem, identify it, study alternative solutions—such as more wastebaskets—but don't train when nontraining solutions can be found.[4]

For our purposes, however, let's accept the fact that nothing can be done *but* train the staff to hit wastebaskets. Here is one approach to the procedure for instructional development.

Step	*Activity*
Analyze the task	During this step, some of the things you need to determine are: What is the difference between a good and poor performer? Why is a good performer good? What are the different conditions under which the paper wads will be thrown? You are, in fact, noting all the things that must be done, and under what conditions, such as locations of open windows, deflecting walls, and air ducts, and you list the differences between successful and poor performers.
Prepare objectives and tests	At this point, you determine what the boss has decided is acceptable performance and prepare a performance test that will demonstrate that the students meet these standards. You also prepare the objectives that describe what they must be able to do, how well, and under what conditions. Your objective may read something like this: Given ten various sized wads of paper, and a 12-inch diameter wastebasket placed 10 feet away against a plastered wall, the student will be able to sink at least eight of ten paper wads. Please note that some decisions have already been made regarding media—at least for the testing phase.

[4]Robert F. Mager and Peter Pipe, *Analyzing Performance Problems* (Belmont, Calif.: Fearon Publishers, 1970).

Refine objectives, select media, and prepare materials

Now you begin breaking the overall objective down into smaller objectives in order to teach those skills that separated the good throwers from the bad. Your lesson content may need to teach such things as: how to check for open windows or hot air drafts; how to discriminate between the weights of different sizes of paper wads; how to hold paper wads, and how to judge distance to the basket, and wad entry angle into it. Here again, some media decisions must be made in order to communicate the lesson content effectively. Decisions must be made on how to distribute the material in the most practical manner, what media can best demonstrate, prompt, inform, provide practice, and give feedback to the students, as well as fit the constraints of your budget and facilities.

Test the materials and revise as necessary

During this step you take your rough lesson material and test it, with the cheapest, most flexible medium or media available, on a small group of *representative* students. You have intentionally *undertaught* material so that you can later add instruction in places where students fail to perform. Remember, you can always find out what you didn't teach, but you will never know what you overtaught. The same principle holds true for the medium or media used to present the instruction. Too often we assume that the lesson requires a more expensive and exotic medium than it really needs.

So you continue to revise and test and revise again, until the lesson finally works—the students achieve the objective, an acceptable level of performance.

Present the training

Now you're ready to conduct the training and make the boss happy. During this phase you not only follow up on the lesson results frequently to make final adjustments, but you also pray a lot.

Now that the wastebasket performance problem is solved successfully, it is time to explain the process used in this guide to assist you in selecting and developing media for instruction.

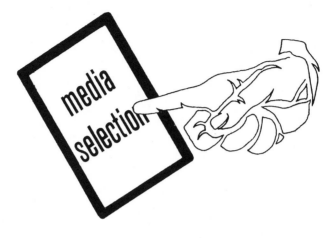

2 The Media Selection Process

Sometimes, of course, the problem of selecting the optimum medium for an instructional program is eliminated by the phrasing of the training request. "We need a video tape on. . ." or "a slide-tape unit should be made for the course on. . ." are statements that replace one problem with another. The statement implies that several essential steps in the process of course development have been completed: need for training has been clearly established; student population has been analyzed and defined; content and objectives have been specified; *and* the medium has been selected on the basis of some judgmental decisions. Implicit, for example, is that this recommendation for a specific medium is based upon careful thought about the most efficient and effective instructional vehicle available and best suited for production, distribution, and utilization within the organization. Unfortunately, such important considerations are not always the basis for selection of media at the time of the initial request, and so the course developer's or instructor's efforts are often seriously impeded.

In contrast to imposed decisions about media at the outset of planning, this book presents a logical series of steps for the selection process. The procedures for the process are based upon *a series of questions that relate course objectives and content with alternative media characteristics.*

9

The questions posed are on a series of media choices in order to narrow the number of alternatives by reasonable decisions. To further narrow your choices, you refer to another *set of questions about a particular selected group of media* based upon such conditions as local production capabilities, facilities, and budgets. Finally, the selection decision is again refined on the basis of the results of developmental testing, which guides acceptance—or revision and retesting—of the medium and materials.

The process is not cumbersome and it is systematic. Practice in its use will make continual reference to the questions less and less necessary. And the process is based, to a degree, on the kinds of decisions we use naturally in daily life when we need to communicate with others.

We may choose to telephone, write a letter, or have face-to-face communication with another person, and the choice is usually based upon a number of variables that we analyze almost automatically. We may choose to call someone on the telephone in order to get instant information about how our remarks are received in order to stress or modify our presentation; or, if we need to have an absolutely clear and verifiable record of what we are saying, we probably write a letter and keep a copy for comparison with the reply. Sometimes to ensure accurate communication, we include visuals such as photographs, drawings, and maps, or, if sound is important to communication, we include audio tapes. If we repeat a message often, we improve on its delivery as we gain experience with the responses of our correspondents or our audience, a form of developmental testing.

The selection of appropriate media for instructional purposes is an extension of this communication skill. It is made more elaborate and somewhat more complicated only because of the need for specific and measurable outcomes that are the result of the instructional communication. Thus, the selection process presented here is given structure to insure inclusion of necessary decisions.

OVERVIEW OF THE SELECTION PROCESS

Please read the overview chart and the explanatory paragraphs on pages 16–17. Follow through each path until you feel confident you understand the structure of the process.

STEP BY STEP THROUGH THE PROCESS

In order to help you better understand the entire selection process, you will now be taken through the series of charts for a situation requiring the use of instructional *media*. With a situation calling for instructional *aids*, a similar process would be used; the only difference would be that in Step 3 you would use Charts 1A and 1B, instead of Charts 1C and 1D, which we will use now.

As you go through this process, you will recognize that the charts are designed to serve as job-aids, and you may use them again and again as you develop instructional units and courses.

Now, look at Chart 1 on page 19. Please familiarize yourself with its content before continuing. You will note that the first thing you do is to take practical action—you make a decision that starts you well on your way.

Information or Instruction?—Step 1

Step (1) determines whether the purpose of the project is *information* or *instruction*.

For practical purposes, we placed all communication projects in one of two categories: *information* (in which we may include entertainment), or *instruction*. Both of these categories have sufficiently different characteristics to suggest that different media may be justified for each. Though course developers are not normally called upon to produce information programs, they may be at times! For example: a generalized presentation is required occasionally to inform management or other persons about a new instructional program; or you may be tagged to do some other form of special report. Because of differences in purposes, the type of message you are to present is likely to affect the media selection.

The principal differences between information and instruction programs are these:

Information	*Instruction*
The receivers of the information are not held responsible for measurable, specific actions or performance. Often the presentation is general in content, and is to give an overview of ideas or subject matter. Purpose may be to generate interest, to give background information, or to promote an idea. (If the receivers are to take responsible action, the program approaches an instructional purpose.)	The receivers of the instruction are to give demonstrable proof that they have learned. Course writers and/or instructors and students are held responsible for the success of the instructional program; and all have evidence of the results.

Without further discussion, keep in mind that there are many informational programs that might have been vastly improved in their return to their sponsors if they had been planned and produced through instructional development procedures and had included some means of feedback.

Determining Transmission Method—Step 2

Many designers of instructional development systems would prefer to put this consideration later in the process, but, because of typical practices in business and industrial training, this decision may be strongly directed by institutional practices or policy. If the latter is true, then the question becomes: Does the organization in which you work have a training center that has formal courses, a staff of instructors, and a policy of teacher-centered instruction? That is, do teachers lecture, give demonstrations, lead class discussions, set up student activities with continual and close instructor supervision? If this is the case, then you will be likely to seek *instructional aids*, that is, media that are designed and produced to be used by the instructor in teaching. The overhead projector would be an example of a piece of equipment typically and widely used as an instructional aid; some other examples are slides, maps, graphs, flip charts, and chalkboards. Instructional aids, then, are media and equipment used to help an instructor to produce learning. But if your organization provides instructional materials for many students scattered over a wide area and in many locations, you most likely would use the second form of resources, *instructional media*.

Instructional media are those media that provide a direct link between the work of the course developer and the student. Generally, with this use of instructional media, the role of an instructor is vastly different from that of a stand-up teacher. When using instructional media, the role of the teacher is usually that of a course monitor, administrator, counselor, and supervisor. Most student work is undertaken by self-direction and by the guidance provided within the instructional media themselves. In some instances, the instructor also serves as an evaluator, especially when performance testing is fundamental in the instruction.

With these evident differences in the types of instruction just described, you can readily understand why the use of the two terms—*aids* and *media*—are justified. Thus, it is important that the decision on the method of instruction should be made early in instructional planning.

Combinations of instructional methods are not to be overlooked, however, and you may be involved in courses in which both instructional aids and instructional media are used. Therefore, you may be using the references from both the green and the red columns in the charts.

Note that the boxes in each column are similar, and that there are only three charts on each side to be used for references.

By arbitrarily choosing instructional media, let's examine the next steps. Turn to Chart 1C, Instructional Media (pages 24–25), and familiarize yourself with its content before we continue with Step 3.

Determining Lesson Characteristics—Step 3

An assumption is made here that you have worked through the preliminary steps in instructional development; you have analyzed the need for training, determined broad goals for the instruction, and written with great care the instructional objectives. Further, you have selected the ways you will determine that learning is achieved by the students.

You will note at the top left entry lane in the chart that you are guided to review your lesson objectives, and the content you have selected, and you decide whether and to what extent the proposed learning is cognitive (knowledge and facts; rules, principles, discriminations, and others you may identify). If an objective is clearly in terms of cognitive learning, then you are directed to other questions. Note that psychomotor (skill) learning objectives will direct you to the same first question: Does the lesson involve objects or things unfamiliar to the student? If YES, then you are directed to Step 3, Chart 1D. Please turn to Chart 1D (pages 26–27) and familiarize yourself with it before going on.

As you work your way down through the questions that relate to the needs of your lesson material, you are asked questions that relate to your lesson content: Is motion necessary? Sound? Real things? Color? When you reach the bottom of Chart 1D, you have arrived at Step 4.

Select an Initial Class of Media—Step 4

For Step 4 you will turn to Chart 2 (page 29). Examine this chart until you are familiar with the classes and the types of items in the columns; in this exercise, of course, use the red column, "Instructional Media."

Here again, for practical considerations, the media have been classified arbitrarily, generally based on their characteristics. Each medium has a number of characteristics, including special capabilities and limitations, according to the quality and type of communication you are expecting of it. Some media are especially capable of presenting information in graphic forms; others are also able to communicate with graphics, but can also add an element of motion, for example, changing colors and guide symbols appearing and disappearing. There are media that are especially made to provide sound. Some media seem to involve the learner more easily than others, and make possible time and opportunity for active responses and performance demonstrations. Some media are especially economical in presenting verbal information, and some, nonverbal graphic information, and some are especially convenient to produce, modify, and revise, or to package and distribute. For a few minutes, study Chart 2 and note the media classifications in the left column. Go back to the top and read across: "I. Audio only. Instructional Media/Instructional Aid." Remember we suggested that this is an arbitrary classification. Also remember that the process with this chart is limited by the author's own experiences and background. You may see immediately a way a medium can and probably should be used after you have gone through Chart 1D and you may well be right—in your situation. So please look upon this system as an aid for you—a course writer and planner—and not as cast in bronze. If it stimulates your imagination to new alternatives, all this work has been worthwhile. Your process of deciding what medium to use for an *instructional* situation has been simplified—and your choices have been narrowed.

Additional help is provided for you in the remaining section of this book, that deals with various specific media.

Analysis of Media Characteristics—Step 5

As each medium is discussed, you will find pages that analyze the instructional capabilities and limitations of the medium to help you reconsider your decision. You should read these pages at the time you arrive at the end of Step 5 to help you decide finally upon the particular medium or media to use. You may often find an alternative choice that is simpler to use, or more economical, or within your immediate capability for production. Turn to pages 108–110 and read the material there about printed material, or to pages 56–57 and read about slides. Note how the analysis can help you as you study your objectives, and later, as you consider the several media recommended for consideration.

As you read the reference pages named above, and as you explore other media, note pertinent considerations that are basic to selecting one or another medium, for a particular training responsibility.

Now, please turn to the final step, developmental testing, which follows the charts.

OVERVIEW OF THE SELECTION PROCESS

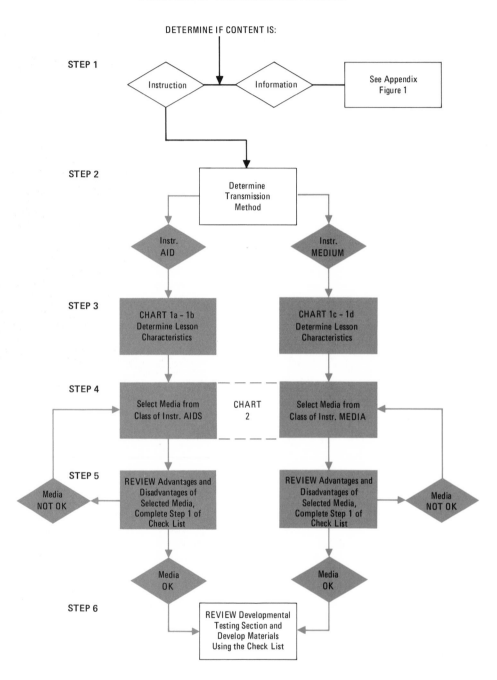

Overview of the Selection Process

On the opposite page is a flowchart of the entire selection process. With the explanations below, you can walk through the series of six steps, which require you to work with, at most, three of the charts.

Step 1.
(Chart 1)

You decide whether your message is instruction or information.

Step 2.
(Chart 1)

Determines how you are to transmit the message—whether it is a medium or media to support an instructor or a medium or media to provide either self-paced or group-paced instruction, without an instructor.

Step 3.
(Charts 1a-1b or 1c-1d)

Using either Charts 1a and 1b or Charts 1c and 1d, you will be assisted in determining the characteristics of your lesson to further narrow your choices of media and to lead you to selecting a specific class of media that is appropriate for your instructional purposes.

Step 4.
(Chart 2)

You will turn to Chart 2 to select a promising medium from the class indicated—one that seems to suit your local production capacities, facilities, policies, and budget.

Step 5.

You refer to your initial choice of medium and review the lists of unique characteristics of that medium and its advantages and disadvantages for presenting the lesson material.

If the medium still seems appropriate, you then complete the last section of the check list, which forces you to review and further refine your selection; the questions here relate to lesson content and objectives.

But, if after these refinements of selection you find the medium no longer seems appropriate, go back to Step 4 and make another choice from the same list. Again, review the check list for that medium, and repeat the process until you are satisfied that the medium is appropriate and meets your conditions for instruction.

Step 6.
(Pages 33 to 34)

Having selected the most feasible medium for your purposes, you then start Step 6—to plan the developmental testing of the medium and your lesson materials.

Note: If you have been assigned a project that clearly has an informational purpose, then refer to the "Appendix," Figures 1 and 2, "Selecting Media for Informational Purposes," for assistance.

CHART 1

MEDIA SELECTION

STEP 1: DETERMINE IF YOU NEED TO PROVIDE <u>INSTRUCTION</u> OR <u>INFORMATION</u>

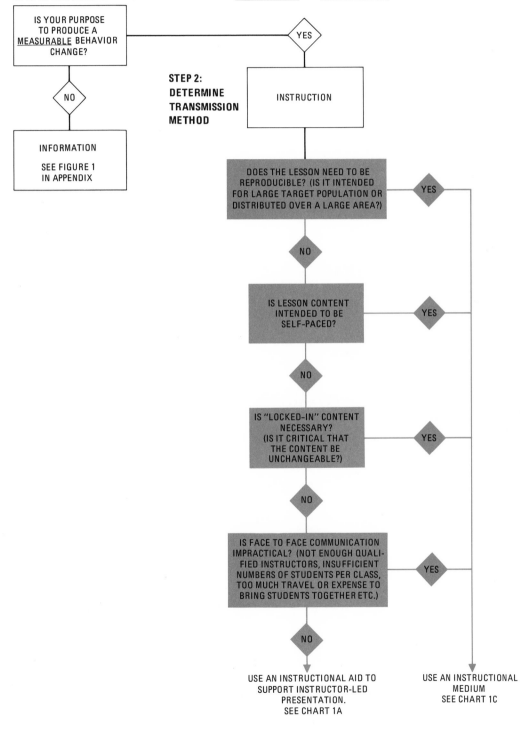

IS YOUR PURPOSE TO PRODUCE A <u>MEASURABLE</u> BEHAVIOR CHANGE?

YES

NO

STEP 2: DETERMINE TRANSMISSION METHOD

INSTRUCTION

INFORMATION

SEE FIGURE 1 IN APPENDIX

DOES THE LESSON NEED TO BE REPRODUCIBLE? (IS IT INTENDED FOR LARGE TARGET POPULATION OR DISTRIBUTED OVER A LARGE AREA?)

YES

NO

IS LESSON CONTENT INTENDED TO BE SELF-PACED?

YES

NO

IS "LOCKED-IN" CONTENT NECESSARY? (IS IT CRITICAL THAT THE CONTENT BE UNCHANGEABLE?)

YES

NO

IS FACE TO FACE COMMUNICATION IMPRACTICAL? (NOT ENOUGH QUALI-FIED INSTRUCTORS, INSUFFICIENT NUMBERS OF STUDENTS PER CLASS, TOO MUCH TRAVEL OR EXPENSE TO BRING STUDENTS TOGETHER ETC.)

YES

NO

USE AN INSTRUCTIONAL AID TO SUPPORT INSTRUCTOR-LED PRESENTATION. SEE CHART 1A

USE AN INSTRUCTIONAL MEDIUM SEE CHART 1C

CHART 1A

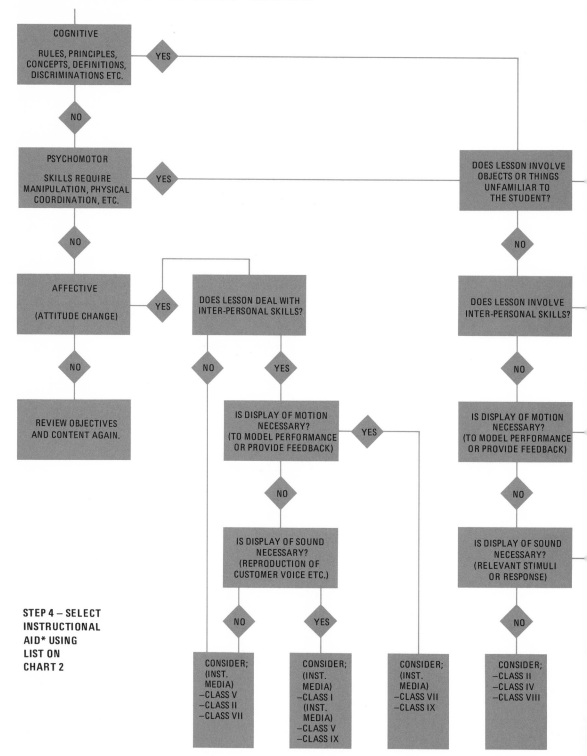

STEP 3 – DETERMINE LESSON CHARACTERISTICS

CONSIDER LESSON OBJECTIVES AND CONTENT – LEARNING IS:

INSTRUCTIONAL AIDS

COGNITIVE

RULES, PRINCIPLES, CONCEPTS, DEFINITIONS, DISCRIMINATIONS ETC.

YES

NO

PSYCHOMOTOR

SKILLS REQUIRE MANIPULATION, PHYSICAL COORDINATION, ETC.

YES

NO

DOES LESSON INVOLVE OBJECTS OR THINGS UNFAMILIAR TO THE STUDENT?

NO

AFFECTIVE

(ATTITUDE CHANGE)

YES

DOES LESSON DEAL WITH INTER-PERSONAL SKILLS?

NO

DOES LESSON INVOLVE INTER-PERSONAL SKILLS?

NO

NO

YES

NO

REVIEW OBJECTIVES AND CONTENT AGAIN.

IS DISPLAY OF MOTION NECESSARY? (TO MODEL PERFORMANCE OR PROVIDE FEEDBACK)

YES

IS DISPLAY OF MOTION NECESSARY? (TO MODEL PERFORMANCE OR PROVIDE FEEDBACK)

NO

NO

IS DISPLAY OF SOUND NECESSARY? (REPRODUCTION OF CUSTOMER VOICE ETC.)

IS DISPLAY OF SOUND NECESSARY? (RELEVANT STIMULI OR RESPONSE)

STEP 4 – SELECT INSTRUCTIONAL AID* USING LIST ON CHART 2

NO

YES

NO

CONSIDER;
(INST. MEDIA)
–CLASS V
–CLASS II
–CLASS VII

CONSIDER;
(INST. MEDIA)
–CLASS I
(INST. MEDIA)
–CLASS V
–CLASS IX

CONSIDER;
(INST. MEDIA)
–CLASS VII
–CLASS IX

CONSIDER;
–CLASS II
–CLASS IV
–CLASS VIII

* UNLESS IDENTIFIED AS INSTRUCTIONAL MEDIA, ALL SELECTIONS ARE FROM CLASS OF INSTRUCTIONAL AIDS

CHART 1A Continued

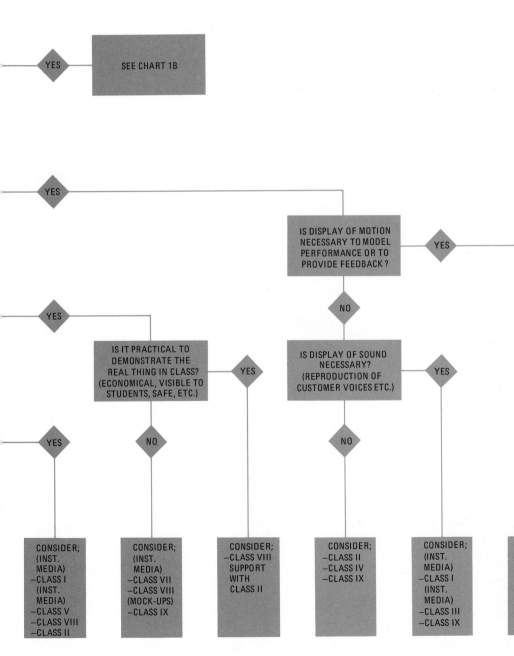

Chart 1B

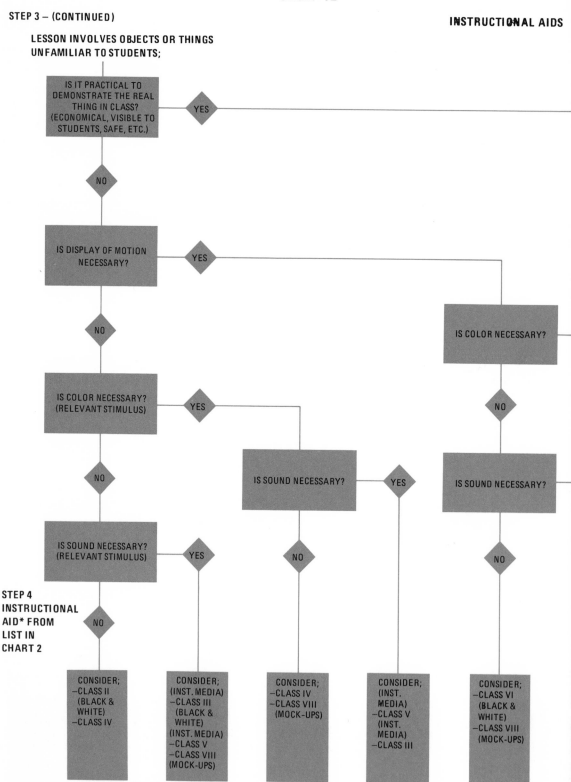

STEP 3 – (CONTINUED)

LESSON INVOLVES OBJECTS OR THINGS UNFAMILIAR TO STUDENTS;

IS IT PRACTICAL TO DEMONSTRATE THE REAL THING IN CLASS? (ECONOMICAL, VISIBLE TO STUDENTS, SAFE, ETC.)

YES

NO

IS DISPLAY OF MOTION NECESSARY?

YES

NO

IS COLOR NECESSARY? (RELEVANT STIMULUS)

YES

NO

IS COLOR NECESSARY?

NO

IS SOUND NECESSARY?

YES

IS SOUND NECESSARY?

NO

IS SOUND NECESSARY? (RELEVANT STIMULUS)

YES

STEP 4
INSTRUCTIONAL
AID* FROM
LIST IN
CHART 2

NO

CONSIDER;
–CLASS II (BLACK & WHITE)
–CLASS IV

CONSIDER;
(INST. MEDIA)
–CLASS III (BLACK & WHITE)
(INST. MEDIA)
–CLASS V
–CLASS VIII (MOCK-UPS)

CONSIDER;
–CLASS IV
–CLASS VIII (MOCK-UPS)

CONSIDER;
(INST. MEDIA)
–CLASS V (INST. MEDIA)
–CLASS III

CONSIDER;
–CLASS VI (BLACK & WHITE)
–CLASS VIII (MOCK-UPS)

* UNLESS IDENTIFIED AS INSTRUCTIONAL MEDIA, ALL SELECTIONS ARE FROM CLASS OF INSTRUCTIONAL AIDS

CHART 1B   Continued

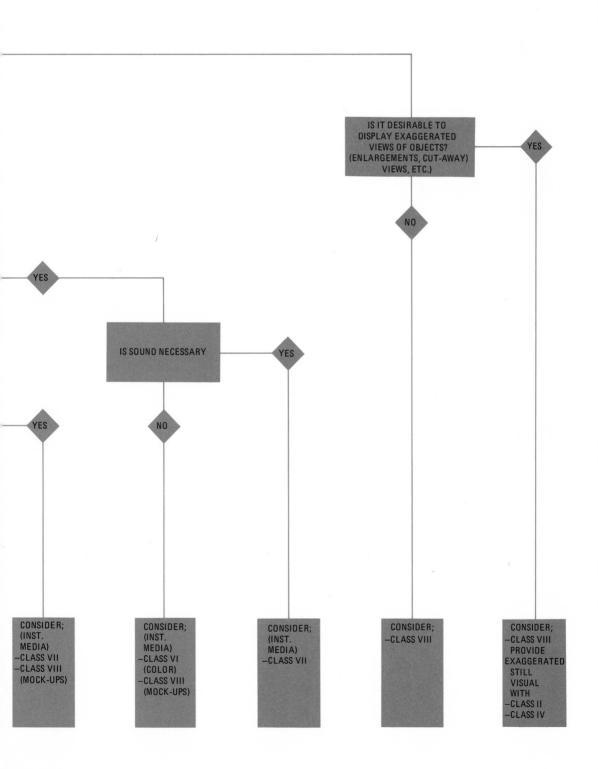

Chart 1C

STEP 3 – DETERMINE LESSON CHARACTERISTICS

INSTRUCTIONAL MEDIA

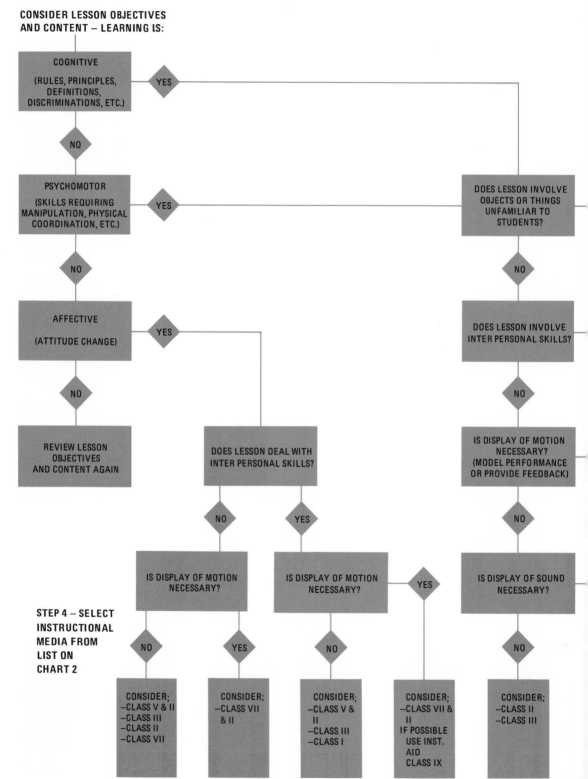

CONSIDER LESSON OBJECTIVES AND CONTENT – LEARNING IS:

COGNITIVE
(RULES, PRINCIPLES, DEFINITIONS, DISCRIMINATIONS, ETC.)

YES

NO

PSYCHOMOTOR
(SKILLS REQUIRING MANIPULATION, PHYSICAL COORDINATION, ETC.)

YES

NO

AFFECTIVE
(ATTITUDE CHANGE)

YES

NO

REVIEW LESSON OBJECTIVES AND CONTENT AGAIN

DOES LESSON DEAL WITH INTER PERSONAL SKILLS?

NO   YES

DOES LESSON INVOLVE OBJECTS OR THINGS UNFAMILIAR TO STUDENTS?

NO

DOES LESSON INVOLVE INTER PERSONAL SKILLS?

NO

IS DISPLAY OF MOTION NECESSARY?
(MODEL PERFORMANCE OR PROVIDE FEEDBACK)

NO

IS DISPLAY OF MOTION NECESSARY?

IS DISPLAY OF MOTION NECESSARY?

YES

IS DISPLAY OF SOUND NECESSARY?

STEP 4 – SELECT INSTRUCTIONAL MEDIA FROM LIST ON CHART 2

NO   YES

NO

NO

CONSIDER;
–CLASS V & II
–CLASS III
–CLASS II
–CLASS VII

CONSIDER;
–CLASS VII & II

CONSIDER;
–CLASS V & II
–CLASS III
–CLASS I

CONSIDER;
–CLASS VII & II
IF POSSIBLE USE INST. AID
CLASS IX

CONSIDER;
–CLASS II
–CLASS III

CHART 1C   Continued

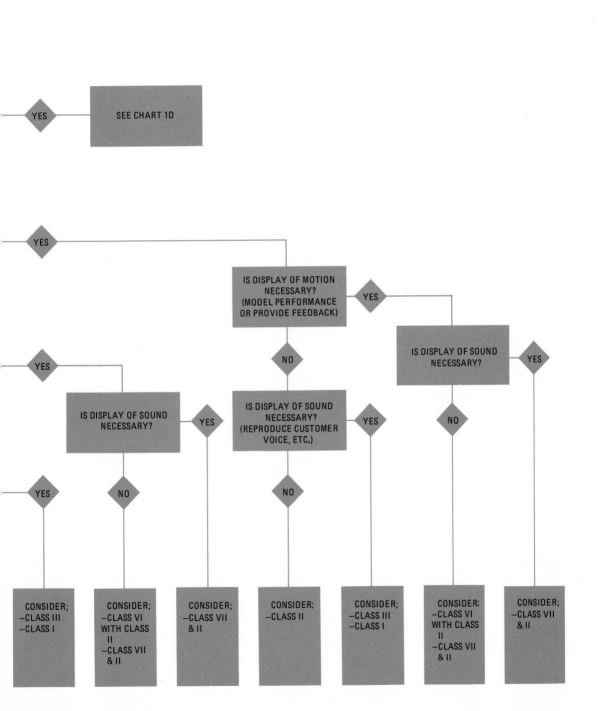

CHART 1D

INSTRUCTIONAL MEDIA

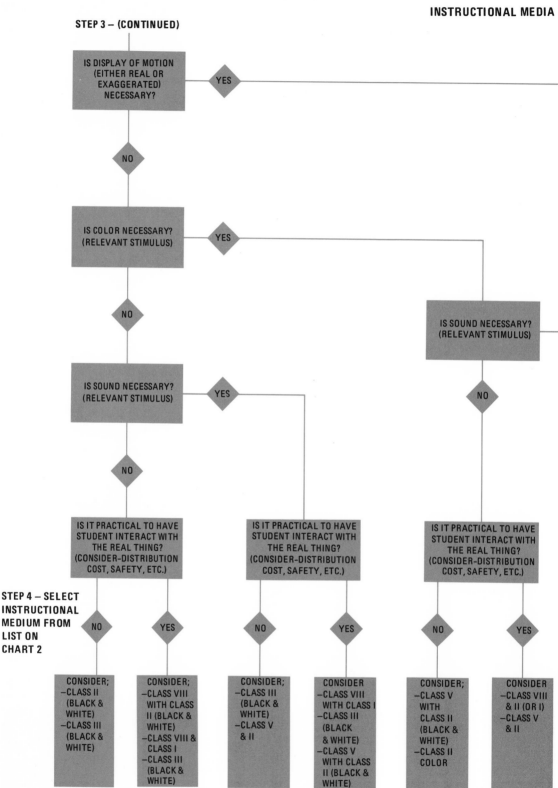

CHARt 1D Continued

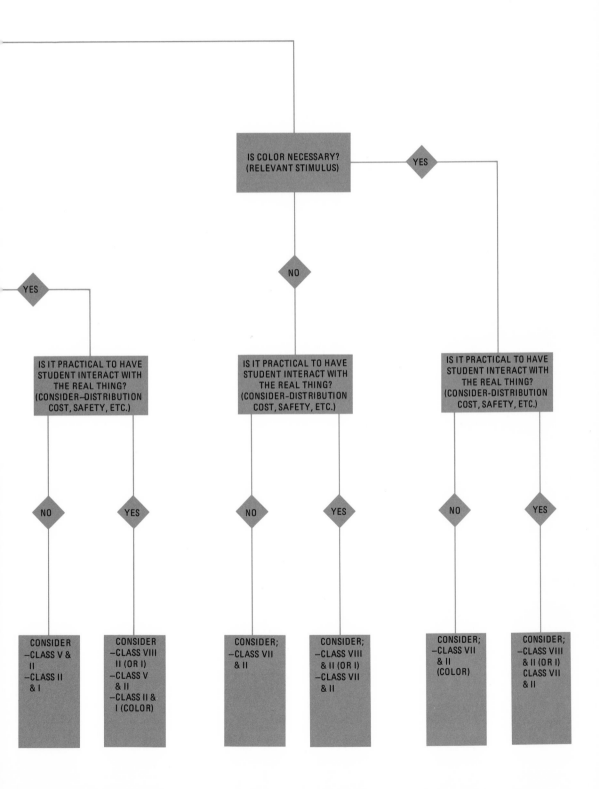

CHART 2

MEDIA CLASSIFICATIONS

MEDIA CLASS	INSTRUCTIONAL MEDIA	INSTRUCTIONAL AID
I. AUDIO (Sound only)	— Audio Tape (reel to reel) (Cassette) — Audio disc — Radio (generally recorded "one-way" transmission)	— Telephone ("Live" person) — Radio (used in "two-way" dialogue)
II. PRINTED MATERIAL (All types of printed matter — including drawings and photographs)	— Programmed texts — Manuals —Job-aids	— Hand-outs — Easels — Chalkboards — Charts, graphs, maps etc. used by instructor
III. AUDIO-PRINT (Combination of Class I & II)	— Student Workbook and audio tape or disc. — Forms, charts, reference materials etc. used with audio tape or disc.	—
IV. PROJECTED STILL-VISUAL	— Slides and Film strips (when supported by recorded verbal message)	— Slides — Transparencies — Film strips — Holograms
V. AUDIO-PROJECTED STILL — VISUAL	— Sound filmstrip (Audio tape or disc and film strip) — Sound slide set (Slides of all types with audio tape or disc)	—
VI. MOTION-VISUAL	— Silent — Motion Film (with captions)	— Silent movie film
VII. AUDIO-MOTION VISUAL	— Motion Picture Film Video (recorded)	— Picturephone Video (conference) Video (instant play back)
VIII. PHYSICAL OBJECTS	— Actual objects — Mock-ups or models of the "real things"	— Actual objects — Mock-ups or models of the "real things"
IX. HUMAN AND SITUATIONAL RESOURCES (Teachers, peers, environment)	—	— Role play situations — Case studies using group members — Group participation in decision making — Field trips
X. COMPUTERS	CAI-CMI — Computers and various terminal display equipment	—

3 Developmental Testing—Step 6

The last step in the media selection process described here is the developmental testing of lesson materials. This phase provides an opportunity to test the numerous decisions and assumptions you have made as you developed the lesson objectives and content, and selected the media for the course. Your purpose is to be sure you have made the right decisions—that your instruction has produced the desired learning—and you have proof of your success. Of course, you also learn where and to what extent your planning may have included *wrong* decisions, and you have an opportunity to repair any inadequacies in your course before you send it to the field. In effect, you are checking to see whether your students behave as you hoped and predicted they would behave as they "take your course."

Many leaders in the field of instruction—Geary Rummler, Peter Pipe, and others—have advocated the use of *lean programming* of lesson materials. Lean programming is accomplished by intentionally overestimating student background and skills and, therefore, carefully underteaching the content of the course; thus, students will reveal where and to what degree you must increase the amount of teaching you must provide. This process is essential to be sure that your course can bring students to the level of competence specified in your objectives.

There are other benefits of developmental testing. You will often find that you have saved student (and company) time, and you have reduced the cost of training. Elimination of student frustration with studying what is already known is another rewarding by-product of this phase.

Lean programming applies, of course, to the development of media: by overestimating student skills and background in the subject, you consciously plan to produce lesson content in media that give fewest possible visual and audio-visual displays and in the forms you consider minimal in cost and complexity. When you test the effectiveness of each part of the course, the developmental process gives you opportunity to revise and increase the amount of media presentations *only* when the student test results indicate that a different or more complex, and expensive, approach is warranted. A good maxim to follow when testing media and instructional procedures is: If it works, leave it alone! This holds true, not only for the quantity of material presented to students, but for the quality of the display as well.

Therefore, during the initial stages of course development it may be a waste of time and money to produce completely finished materials of high technical quality. Frequently much of the instructional material produced at the start of production development will survive and will be incorporated in the final product. If materials must be discarded or heavily revised, however, low cost initial media are more likely to be put aside with minimal regret. For practical purposes, both instructional and economic, do not commit yourself to expensive initial media production. Keep developmental phases of production flexible, economical, and simple, and be guided by developmental testing for necessary revisions.

In the following material, some procedures are suggested for completing the media selection and development process during the developmental testing phase of your instructional program. Two tests are outlined, along with hints for conducting the testing. Additional refinements in testing procedures will depend upon your growing skill and ingenuity as a course developer and your growing background in test and evaluation procedures.

HINTS FOR TESTING MEDIA DURING COURSE DEVELOPMENT

General

If possible, leave an obvious error in the beginning of the lesson to allow the student to criticize the material and feel more relaxed and comfortable during the testing.

If the test is in performance, put the student at ease by showing confidence in his abilities.

Note carefully during testing where the student appears to be bored, distracted, or confused and bogged down. Later, ask about these apparent problems.

Don't rush to the aid of any student when confusion or perplexity seems evident. Take notes, and discuss any problems later. Always encourage students to ask questions if they feel the need, and make notes privately of questions asked; seek clues for revising either test or course.

Experiment to seek the least complex media available to achieve course purposes. For example, if possible use only one medium—audio or visual— to determine if required student performance is achieved; if it is, you probably don't need a more complicated audio-visual presentation.

In a private, post test session, ask each student—without reference to course material—to recall important parts of the lesson. Verify whether their identification of important points matches the intent of the course. Edit or revise the course and the media if necessary.

Developmental Test 1

Select the cheapest, most flexible medium available that *approximates* what you have considered as a final medium for instruction.

Final Product	*Approximation Test Material*
Audio Materials	Typed copy of script to be read by student. Cassette copy of script to be narrated by developer.
Printed Materials	Duplicated copies of handwritten or rough typed materials. Hand printed easel sheets or printing on chalk boards. If binders are *necessary* use reusable looseleaf binders.
Audio and Printed Materials	Combination of approximations noted above.
Projected Still Visuals (slides, filmstrips, transparencies).	Pencil sketches of intended visuals. Simple drawings and typed words on negative (Koda-lith) slides. Simple drawings and handwritten words on overhead transparencies. Black and white prints (Polaroid) pasted on sheets or cards.
Audio and Projected Still Visuals	Combination of approximations noted above.

Film/Video	Simple drawings and printed narration on story-boards.
	Simple visual drawings with audio narrated on cassette by developer.
	Rehearsal video tape using local talent and produced with portable VTR unit.
	Filmograph—video or film of still pictures—motion simulated by camera or movement of the art or photos.

Developmental Test 2

After materials have been revised, based on the results of Test 1, continue to test using materials produced in closer approximation to the final product.

Final Product	*Approximation*
Audio Material	A cassette tape incorporating script changes and narrated by the course developer.
Printed Material	Same as Test 1. Typed clean copy of materials incorporating revisions. Use simple line drawings or black and white photographs.
Audio and Printed Materials	Revised copies of approximates noted above.
Projected Still Visuals (slides, filmstrips, transparencies).	Simple drawings on negative slides. Slides shot on location or on copy stand.
Audio and Projected Still Visuals	Audio tape narrated by course developer, accompanied by slides. (If slides are ultimately to be changed automatically by synchronized tape, add an audible cue, gong, or clunk on the tape during narration recordings to indicate slide change.)
Film/Video	Slides and audio tape (narrated by writer). Revised run-through of rehearsal quality, video tape using local talent and portable VTR unit.

Continue to edit and revise the lesson materials until testing proves the desired student performance is achieved. When ready to field test the final product, use the final product or the closest possible approximation. There is no clear cut rule for this final testing procedure, and every case may be different, depending on the attitudes of the intended students and their supervisors, the cost of the media production, and the likelihood of revisions.

As indicated earlier, any further refinements in testing and selection will be left to the skill of the individual developer, and will vary according to the time available for testing, the cooperation of students, and the ingenuity of the developer. Again, a reminder. *If it works, leave it alone!*

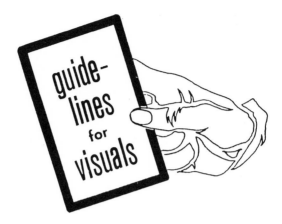

4 Guidelines for Visuals

Sight is by far the most powerful of the senses through which we perceive the world around us. Research supports this flat statement, although the relative contribution of sight in comparison to the other senses seems to vary according to numerous circumstances. Nevertheless, in this discussion we accept as fact that almost all people depend upon sight as their primary source of information. People are generally conditioned to keep their visual sense occupied during most waking hours. They continually watch for information, cues, alarms, and items of interest. This primacy of sight has important implications for teaching and learning.

The visual channel *must* be considered by course developers when planning training strategy and in developing course materials. If the course developer doesn't plan to use the visual sense, something or someone else will. There is always the exception, of course: an exceptional person—an orator, perhaps—can catch and maintain audience attention for long periods of time, but these rare people have a special talent for generating visual imagery in the minds of their audiences. But even the golden-tongued orator might find it difficult to keep an audience attentive if he were to lecture on the history of the drill press without some visual assistance.

Think of your experiences listening to lecturers who talked *at* you, thus failing to command your visual sense. When the sense of hearing *only* is bombarded, whether by a live lecturer or a voice on an audio tape, you—or any audience—will become distracted. Students avoid such punishment by sleeping (turning off the senses of sight and sound) or daydreaming (allowing irrelevant images, real or imaginary, to occupy the mind).

The visual sense is highly discriminating, constantly analyzing visual events to accept or reject new information based upon what is already known. Any visual image that conflicts with our own real world may be summarily rejected and may, thus, present a barrier to learning.

Sight is sensitive to punishment. Generally we are unwilling to tolerate any strain, including illegible or ambiguous visual images or sudden and extreme changes in illumination. We are also inclined to turn off shocking or boring visual displays.

Although materials in books and other forms of print are not of *principal* concern here, visuals are continually used in all kinds of printed matter. The characteristics of printed type displays and page layouts can be motivational and effective in communicating to students, or they may confuse, bore, or punish.

Therefore, be alert to the problems that may arise because the sense of sight may be mistreated in any instructional presentation to the detriment of student learning.

Here, then, are some rules of thumb to consider when you are designing visuals for instruction. Remember, these are neither laws nor absolutes, but reminders for you. As you conduct developmental testing of your programs, watch for causes of failures because you may have failed to observe one or more of these guidelines.

SOME RULES OF THUMB FOR VISUALS

*Visuals used simultaneously with audio materials **must** be directly relevant to the audio content.*

If the audio presentation carries the principal weight of the content, visuals can inhibit learning if:

- they conflict with what is being presented verbally;
- trivial visuals are used; for example, a visual used just to have something on the screen, or, a simple, instantly grasped visual is left on the screen while the verbal presentation goes on and on, beyond the content of the visual;
- flashy, arty visuals are presented to impress or challenge the viewer; but, the student may be diverted to irrelevant thoughts or emotional reactions.

Excessive redundancy between visual and audio components should be avoided.

- If words are visually displayed, the viewers should be given time to read them before the narrator comments or rephrases the projected message.

- If the print on the screen is brief, group reading can be controlled by having the narrator repeat the printed words exactly. But reserve identical or parroted visual and audio verbiage for very brief and important messages to be stressed. Consider the procedure the same as underlining.

*Visual displays should **not** be punishing.*

- Projected visuals must be legible to minimize student discomfort and frustration. Both clarity and brightness of images are involved in legibility.

  Visuals should not be ambiguous, which means:

- as early in the lesson as possible, unfamiliar objects should be displayed in relation to familiar objects to provide information about size and shape; and

- visuals should not be busy or cluttered, to ensure that the intended communication is clear to the viewers.

Visuals should not be distasteful to students or to any audience.

- Since we are assuming that we want to encourage people to change their behavior in desirable ways, we don't want to alienate them; quite the opposite, we want to encourage them and attract them to the subject. Therefore, display of scenes that some students find either morally or emotionally shocking should be avoided or, at least, used with great care, and the results checked. You may have objectives that you believe can be met only by jolting your audience; in such cases you may have serious problems. Use even humor with care and judgment, and test the results.

  Because motion visuals (film and video) are generally considered effective media for producing attitudinal changes, and because they are also expensive, errors in judgment in their use can be deeply regretted.

Visuals representing on-the-job situations must be acceptably realistic.

  All instructional situations should:

- accurately reflect company or institutional policies and practices in such matters as dress, demeanor, work and safety rules, and models of performance;

- show views of persons using tools, instruments, and control equipment, for examples, from the point of view of the person using them on the job. Work environments and situations should, to the greatest degree possible, represent the real world. This does not mean that lesson materials and the learning environment must be exact replicas of reality to effect desired learning, but conditions representing typical factors that control performance of personnel should be provided.

Projected visual materials are usually designed to be displayed in a horizontal format.

- The lower portion of viewing screens in many classrooms is difficult to see from back rows of seats. To overcome this problem, design visuals in horizontal format to keep the bottom of the image as high as possible.

- Students have been conditioned by the media used for entertainment to expect horizontal visuals. Avoid including an occasional vertical format in a series of horizontal visuals—it can be distracting.

- Motion pictures, both film in all sizes and video, have a horizontal format and the proportions are not generally altered, except for wide-screen motion pictures or two- or three-screen slide presentations.

Color, unless required for content, usually adds very little to learning.

Guidelines for Legibility for All Projected Visuals *Except Video*

To determine the size of the projected image in relation to the viewing distance, use the **6W** formula:

All projected visuals—excluding video—are based on the premise that 1 foot of screen width is required for each 6 feet of viewing distance from the screen.

This formula is used to determine the proper screen-size-to-room-length ratio in the design of auditoriums and classrooms. For our purposes we will assume that viewing screens or projection walls of adequate size are provided in instructional areas.

Test preliminary artwork or graphics to be projected on the screen *before* they are put on film. Here is the way to make the test:

Measure *in inches* the width of the artwork or lettering display to be projected.

Divide your answer by 2.

Hold the artwork or display that many *feet* away from a viewer and ask him to read the content or to describe the image. If the viewer is successful, your design is adequate for projection.

Example: Your artwork is 10 *inches* wide; divide it by 2 = 5 *inches*. Have the viewer read the display from a distance of 5 *feet*.

Caution: Do not read or test the visual yourself; your memory may help you. Select someone to make the test who is completely unfamiliar with the work, and who has reasonably normal vision.

Image clarity and brightness. It is obvious that the clarity and sharpness of the original artwork or graphic display affects the quality of the reproduced product—whether on film, in print, or on a video screen. No amount of camera magic can turn a poor quality image into a good one. Simply put, the idea is—garbage in, garbage out. One major contributor to unclear, distorted, or even weak visuals is *generation loss*, that is, the degradation of image by duplication. The original quality decreases in each succeeding generation. When working with artwork or graphics to be converted for projection, bear in mind the following:

- Avoid using art or graphics that have apparent flaws. If you think a small smudge or erasure mark won't matter, remember it will be many times more evident when enlarged on a screen.

- When possible, use original artwork or graphics, or slides, to make a master copy, or, for short runs, use the original for making each duplicate.

- If the original artwork is not available, use a first master copy, master slides, film internegative, or filmstrip masters for duplicating. Avoid using release prints or other late generation products for duplicating.

- When working with slides mounted in glass, or slides to be used with rear projection, inform your photographic personnel or laboratory. Frequently they can compensate for these conditions and make adjustments to provide optimum image brightness.

Guidelines for Legibility of Video Materials

To determine the size of the projected image in relation to the viewing distance, use the **12W** formula. For television, the ratio of screen width to viewing distance is different from that for other projected visuals. To test for legibility of visuals intended to be used on video displays follow this procedure:

Measure the width of the artwork or graphic display *in inches*.

Hold the artwork or graphic as many *feet* away from a person or persons selected to test your visuals as the number of inches measured for the art or graphic. If the materials can be read or explained by the viewers, they should be legible when viewed as television images on a well adjusted receiver.

Example: The original artwork or graphic display measures 12 *inches* wide (including the necessary margins); the evaluators will view the material from a distance of 12 *feet*. Be reminded, don't trust yourself as a test subject.

Image clarity and brightness. When working with artwork, graphics, and photographs to be displayed in black and white video, you must consider the color spectrum. For example, some shades of red and green project as similar shades of gray. Learn to use a gray scale, and test all art work with color content on a television system before making finished copy. When planning black and white video productions it is advantageous to:

- Use black and white and shades of gray for artwork and graphics.
- If you must use a colored visual, test it on a portable video unit before final showing. In fact, unless you have much experience, it is best to check *all* visuals on a system with a receiver similar to that to be used by viewers under normal conditions for them. Don't ever use a finely tuned, high-resolution monitor to test visuals.
- Avoid bright, shiny surfaces that can create glare when lighted.
- As with other media, quality reproduction is possible by duplicating from master tape to the same size or smaller tape; avoid, if you can, duplication to tape wider than the original.
- When transferring between film and video, you can usually obtain the best quality by going from film to video, not from video to film. There are, however, special processes that will produce satisfactory results under the opposite conditions, but they are expensive.
- Master tapes should be stored in a cool, safe location, preferably on wood shelves, and racked in a vertical position.

Guidelines for Visual Formats

Visual formats should be understood to avoid problems: although projected visuals should all be designed in horizontal format, the ratio of height to width is not the same for all media. This fact can present problems when the same visuals are to be produced with different media. For example, 35mm slide images are 2 units high by 3 units wide, while 16mm film images are 3 units high by 4 units wide. (See the sample formats, following the summary.) As another example, the format of 35mm slides with a 2:3 ratio is different from the television format, which is 3 units high by 4 units wide (3:4).

Since legibility standards for television are different from those for projected media (see the 6W and 12W formulas), and since visuals originally made for other media must often be used for television productions, the problems that can arise should be anticipated and avoided at the outset of production planning. For example, 35mm slides that have been designed for projection according to the 6W formula probably should be redone for satisfactory presentation on television.

A NOTE IN SUMMARY

These rules are generally applicable to all visual materials. There are, of course, situations that require bending the rules to achieve a desired effect. These occur particularly in the motion-visual field, and in attempts to make training materials for affective-attitudinal objectives. Each situation must be coped with on an individual basis. Unfortunately, there are no cookbook recipes that will guarantee success under all conditions, and we frequently have to compromise. Test, revise, and test; revise again and test again.

When you are developing all types of media for instruction, and especially those that are expensive and sophisticated, the more time spent on preproduction planning, and the more revising and editing of rough-draft materials during developmental testing, the greater the possibility for success. Without sufficient planning, even the most sophisticated medium available will not make poor lesson material good. In fact, the reverse effect may result, and poor material will appear to be even worse than it is.

VISUAL FORMATS

SLIDES
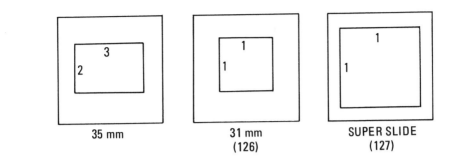

35 mm   31 mm
(126)   SUPER SLIDE
(127)

(FILM)
MOTION PICTURES

FILMSTRIPS
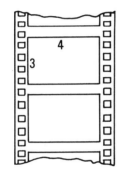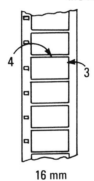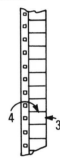

35 mm SINGLE FRAME   16 mm   8 mm

OVERHEAD
TRANSPARENCIES
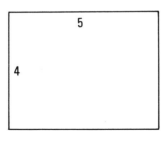

VIDEO
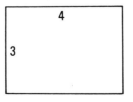

5 Still Visuals

OVERHEAD TRANSPARENCIES

The overhead projector, because it is designed to be operated by an instructor at the front of a class or audience, is a perfect example of an instructional aid. As an aid, the medium is flexible, convenient to use, and, when well used, of great benefit to both the instructor and the students.

The overhead projector is possibly the only widely used piece of instructional equipment that was developed especially for the education field, rather than having been adopted from consumer or commercial entertainment products. Though useful for groups of any size, the overhead projector, was especially developed to project still visual images for a large number of students assembled at one location. Several major advantages of overhead projection explain its increasing use at all levels of education and for many instructional situations: the instructor can face students in a lighted room, and can control the sequence of visual displays during a presentation; elements in a visual can be pointed out, and various techniques permit manipulation of the elements to improve the visual communication.

Preparation of artwork for overhead projection is simple; many instructors prepare their own transparencies, either by hand or with mechanical lettering and drawing techniques, and with a number of available methods for making final transparencies. Drawings made on paper can be made into transparencies on transparent plastic materials by several processes: heat, electrostatic, or diazo. Each of these methods has advantages, but all produce satisfactory images in black and white or in colors.

When using overhead projectors, it is advantageous to project the image on a screen tilted forward at the top to eliminate image distortion called a keystone effect. There are times, however, when it is necessary to project the image on a flat, white wall and still have acceptable results. Viewing area, audience size, and the quality and content of the overhead visuals to be used are all important considerations in selecting projected image size. Judging the legibility characteristics of a transparency by viewing it at hand-held distance, rather than by projection, can be misleading in determining whether the image is appropriately designed for the audience. Review, if you need to, the material on viewing standards in the section "Rules of Thumb for Visuals."

Despite the many advantages of overhead projection, often instructors and program developers tend to use more sophisticated and expensive media devices for instructional aids. Such devices can be effective, but in situations where an instructor is the principal transmitter of lesson content, the overhead projector is often far more effective and dramatically less expensive than the attractive, but complex and costly, alternatives.

In this section, as in the others on various media, guidelines are presented for course developers and instructors in selecting, planning, and producing overhead transparencies for specific purposes during instruction. Topics include: the class of the medium, characteristics, examples of applications, advantages and disadvantages, and check lists of considerations to help you plan the production and use of overhead projection transparencies.

Relating Overhead Transparencies to Instructional Objectives

Class of media: Instructional aid.

Characteristics: Still visual (limited capability for motion or simulated motion.)

Application to types of learning:

Cognitive objectives. Overhead transparencies can be used to teach recognition of, and discrimination among, relevant visual elements. Overhead projection visuals can:

Teach recognition of unfamiliar objects or things by displaying to students visual representations—symbols, pictures, drawings, and forms.

Teach discrimination skills by comparing and contrasting pictured objects, whether shown simultaneously or sequentially. By use of a pointer, directly on the transparency, critical differences among objects can be quickly and accurately indicated on the screen image.

Enhance teaching of discrimination skills by exaggerating differences in objects that may otherwise be overlooked by using line drawings, enlargements, and color coding.

Demonstrate such relationships as interaction of objects in motion, and changes in position by use of simple overlays of translucent, colored materials, or by polarized materials. (Actions, for example, are: parts moving in a pump, pistons in an engine, or the flow of fluids.)

Show principles of operation of objects that normally have working parts enclosed and invisible for observation.

They can also be used to teach rules, principles, or concepts. When used for these purposes, overhead projection can:

Reinforce the comments of an instructor through the use of visual representations of numerical values—percentages, amounts, or ratios—through the use of such graphics as charts, diagrams, and scales.

Display words or phrases to be stressed, or present an outline of points to be shown in coordination with the instructor's presentation.

Clarify and reinforce the instructor's commentary by displaying elements of the lesson content.

Provide visual cues for the instructor to follow in presenting lesson material—a visual outline that helps both instructor and students, and reduces the need for a written script or stacks of notes.

Psychomotor objectives. Limited application. May be used to show positions of things or people in motion before instructor demonstrations or student practice—for example, body positions for lifting heavy weights from the floor, in safety training.

Affective objectives. Generally does not apply.

Advantages and Disadvantages of Overhead Transparencies

Advantages. Overhead projection:

- Allows freedom for an instructor to edit, sequence, and revise instructional material.
- Allows instructors to face an audience in a lighted room to permit interpersonal exchange and to encourage questions and discussion.
- Permits instructors to write on a transparency, and to use a pointer, or to edit items during projection.
- Provides opportunity for simple visuals in black line or in colors, or in combination.

- Permits sequential disclosure of information by adding to an initial base visual using overlays, thus building the display.
- Permits local production of transparencies by the instructor or semi-skilled staff.
- Permits generally inexpensive production of visual materials and, when small quantities are needed for distribution, simple and economical distribution.
- Permits display of transparent or translucent materials on the stage of the projector and enlargements for viewing on the projection screen.
- Permits motion within limits, by translucent plastic cut-outs, or by a more sophisticated and expensive process of using polarized plastic sheets and a hand- or motor-driven polarized rotor in front of the projector lens.
- Offers a variety of portable and permanent projectors with various lenses for adjusting picture size to projector to screen distance requirement.
- Permits adaptation of transparency masters, by plan, for paper prints to be used as handouts or for evaluation purposes.

Disadvantages. Drawbacks are as follows:

- Limited to use as an instructional aid by an instructor or by students for their presentations. Seldom used as an instructional medium.
- Widespread distribution of transparencies individually or in sets may be less convenient than the more compact slides or filmstrips, for example.
- Multicolored, commercially or locally produced transparencies may be more expensive that 35mm slides.
- When using overhead projection, distraction or discomfort may be caused by the flash of unfiltered white light on the screen while changing transparencies.
- Designed for front screen projection, the overhead is seldom used for rear screen projection, except in unusual circumstances.
- If overhead transparency formats are to be transferred to 35mm slides or made into printed paper handouts, special attention must be given to such matters as scale, proportions, lettering size, and border spaces around the pictorial image.
- Often requires a special tilted screen to avoid extreme keystone effect that distorts the visual image.

Check List of Considerations for Selecting and Developing Transparencies for Instruction

How to use the check lists. The following material is divided into five segments, listed in purposeful order, and is to be used *after* the initial decision to use overhead projection has been reached. The lists and activities are intended as mind-joggers to help you plan effectively for the production and use of your visual materials.

Segment A lists questions designed to help you confirm or reevaluate your decision to use overhead projection. Segments B through D are to help you plan the content of the instruction you wish to visualize. Segment E is to help you in ordering the production of visual materials. (It also provides some suggestions for presentation techniques.)

A. Confirm or reevaluate your decision to use overhead projection techniques in the lesson.

	YES	NO
Is the lesson material to be presented by an instructor? (If the answer is NO you should not use this medium.)	____	____
Will *exact* reproduction of the *visual and oral* information be required each time the lesson is presented? If *exact* reproduction is required, you should NOT use this medium; consider, for example, slide-tape techniques instead.	____	____
Is the verbal message to be presented by the instructor long and complex, suggesting that visuals could help the audience concentrate, and fix its attention on an orderly progression of ideas? If NO, consider having the instructor lecture using a few simple handouts.	____	____
Is it easier for students to hear what you want them to know by showing them visual representations of objects or things as they are discussed?	____	____
Are there parts of the verbal message that can better be expressed visually or with visual support material than by words alone? ("One picture is worth a thousand words.")	____	____
Are there parts of the verbal message that need to be stressed by repeating them visually, or are there points to be stressed through a progressive (or sequential?) build up of images?	____	____

B. On separate sheets, make notes that describe briefly the overhead transparency visuals needed. If a lesson outline or script has been developed, indicate on it the locations and code numbers of the visuals planned. (A good way to number is to make your system refer to the page of the outline or script, and to use a code representing the type of medium; also, if more than one visual is listed on a page, provide sequence numbers. Here is one way to do it: The visual number is indicated: T-9-B, where T = Transparency, 9 means page 9, and B means the second visual used. Such a system helps keep visuals in order, and simplifies your numbering problem when you drop or add symbols.)

C. Review the sequence of learning points in the content to determine whether the content should be resequenced either to: improve the logical appeal of the presentation, or, better utilize the visuals. Plan transitions between visuals as well as introductions to visuals, to be as smooth as possible to avoid distractions.

D. Make a sketch of each visual with pencil on 8½ by 11 paper. Check the following questions. All answers should be YES.

	YES	NO
Have you reviewed the section on developmental testing in this book?	___	___
If the lesson deals with objects or things, have you considered whether the students are familiar with them?	___	___
If students are unfamiliar with the objects or things, have you provided visuals that show perspective and size scale, and in different views so that students will recognize the objects or things later on in training or on the job?	___	___
If objects to be shown are tools or equipment that students will use on the job, did you show them over-the-shoulder views as they will see them on the job?	___	___
Have you reviewed the rules of thumb for visuals, in this book to check points that pertain to this project?	___	___
Have you used a horizontal format?	___	___
Are the graphics as simple as possible, yet clearly communicate your ideas?	___	___
Did you check to determine if basic transparencies are already available for use in this lesson?	___	___
Have you planned to use overlays and masks when appropriate to develop cut-away images, progressive disclosures, and identification symbols or words?	___	___
Did you check the visuals for accuracy?	___	___
Did you check for legibility of the visual? (Check again the 6W formula and suggestions for lettering in the section on rules of thumb.)	___	___

Have you avoided overloading the visual with too many details?   —— ——

Did you avoid a busy, cluttered design?   —— ——

Are all the visuals really necessary? Does each one fulfill a planned and useful function in the lesson?   —— ——

Have you resisted using too many visuals in the total lesson, since changing visuals often, and too rapidly, can become distracting both to students and instructor?   —— ——

Is the visual for the audience, not solely for the instructor? (Notes for the instructor should be on the *frame* of the transparency, and not in the projection area.)   —— ——

E. Place an order for production or produce your visuals. When requesting transparencies from your departmental or commercial production sources, check the following questions. All answers should be YES.

	YES	NO
If original artwork is required, is this work clearly described in the order?	——	——
Have you noted colors that are required, and have you indicated exactly where they are to be used?	——	——
If original artwork is required, have you allowed sufficient lead time for the job?	——	——
Have you clearly indicated overlays, their number, the sequence in which they will be used, and any other technical details that require production attention?	——	——

Storage of Transparencies and Masters for Overhead Projection

Store transparencies in protective envelopes or folders. The transparencies will be protected if the folders are used when transporting the visuals. Otherwise, separate transparencies with sheets of paper to avoid abrasion or finger marks.

Avoid exposing transparencies to light and excessive heat for long times, and keep the plastic surfaces clean and free of dust, grit, and finger-prints. Remove completely any color remaining after using removable felt pen markings. Provide clear, blank transparent plastic sheets for instructors who wish to mark on their transparencies; by use of the clear sheet for writing and marking the original transparency will retain original clarity.

Suggestions for Overhead Transparency Presentations

The following information is to help you prepare hints for persons who will use the transparencies in their presentations.

Project on a screen of adequate size, tilted forward at the top sufficiently to avoid an extreme keystone image.

For ease of operation, the overhead projector is best used when the instructor is seated. Place the projector on a low stand alongside a table or desk, with the top of the projector stage at the same level.

Avoid leaving the projector light on the screen while changing visuals, as the glare is distracting.

Use masks, overlays, translucent objects, and pointers (a thin, sharp pencil, a pointed cocktail stirring rod, or a sharp stick).

Provide assistance for instructors who want to learn to use transparencies, and encourage them to practice the presentation privately, before facing a class.

SLIDES

The standard 2″ by 2″ (35mm) slide is probably the most widely used still-visual medium on the market today. It's low production cost, compactness, and versatility appeal to many users and producers of instructional and informational programs. As stated in the section, "Guidelines for Visuals," *all* still visuals, including 35mm slides, are designed to be viewed horizontally. Among novice course developers and instructors, there is a tendency to assume that because it is *possible* to use vertical slide images it is *logical* to do so. Even though a vertical image would ease the legibility problem when photographing original materials such as printed forms, the vertical format poses other problems for both instructors and students in a classroom designed for viewing horizontal images. The horizontal format for slides is strongly recommended.

Several films are produced in a square format, including Super Slides (127 film) and 31mm slides (126 film). However, these slides are rarely used by professional photographers who are required to produce large quantities of projected visuals for industrial or educational institutions.

To the course developer, one of the most compelling reasons to use slides for instruction is that they can serve as both instructional aids to support an instructor's presentation or as an instructional medium when combined with recorded sound. In addition, lesson materials can be rearranged, or substitutions can be made, with minimum delay and maximum economy. However, more examples of the advantages and disadvantages of slides are discussed in the following pages.

The principal purpose of this section, as in each section devoted to an individual medium, is to provide you with simple check lists that you can review when planning and developing visual instructional materials.

Relating Slides to Instructional Objectives

Class of media: Instructional aid *or* instructional medium (when used in conjunction with audio or print).

Characteristics: Still visual (limited and expensive semimotion capability).

Application to types of learning:

Cognitive objectives. Slides can be used to teach recognition and/or discrimination of relevant visual stimuli. For example, slides can:

> Teach recognition of unfamiliar objects or things by displaying visual representations (pictures or drawings).

> Teach discrimination skills by visually contrasting objects shown sequentially or at the same time.

> Enhance the teaching of discrimination skills by exaggerating differences in objects through visuals such as line drawings and enlargements.

> Display principles of objects having internal working parts through the use of cut-away views.

> Present a representation of the working location, position, or situations that the student will face in the real world.

Slides can also be used to teach rules, principles and sequences of events. Thus, they can:

> Reinforce an instructor's presentation through the use of graphic representations such as charts, diagrams, and scales.

> Display words or points to be stressed in the instructor's commentary and thereby provide reinforcement and emphasis.

> Clarify instructor's commentary by also displaying the lesson content.

> Provide visual cues as a guide to the presented materials.

Psychomotor objectives. Little, if any, application. Still-visual displays can point out static positions of moving items, ways to hold items to be manipulated, or other critical incidents in the movement of objects.

Affective objectives. Slides used in combination with audio tapes can carry effective attitude-changing material. Even when well done, slides still rank below motion pictures (film or video) for affective presentations. One especially attractive feature of slide and sound presentations is the relatively low cost of production compared with sound and motion media. However, as with any medium, the cost is low if the program gets results, but expensive if nothing constructive happens to the learner.

Advantages and Disadvantages of Slides

Advantages are as follows:

- Color visuals can be produced economically in slides.
- Slides are reproducible in large quantities.
- The small size of slides allows for: compact packaging and storage; ease of distribution; and convenient transportation for use in various locations.

When slides are used as an instructional aid:

- Instructors can adapt their lessons for different student groups or vary emphasis by deleting, or adding slides before each presentation.
- Instructors can back up visual displays to review specific points.
- The large visual display on a screen allows an instructor to point out critical items.

Slides can also serve as an instructional *medium* when used (in combination with audio or print). For example: A preprogrammed sequence of slides can provide exact visual content that can inhibit the tendency of various presenters or instructors to revise or improvise lessons. The compact size of slides facilitates the production and distribution of individualized lesson materials.

Versatility of display through slides allows for:

- Visuals to be designed for progressive disclosure of information.
- Visuals designed to present special visual effects such as cut-away or enlarged views of objects and distortion of image for impact.
- Economical (and realistic) visual representations of what the student will see in the real world.

Disadvantages. These disadvantageous facts must be weighed as well.

- Effective projection of slides generally requires lighting to be dimmed and controlled for an adequate visual display. Usually this concern presents a problem only when slides are used as an instructional aid.
- Processing is seldom done locally. Depending upon available laboratory services, you must wait from 24 hours to several days for commercial film development and mounting of slides.
- Use of several of the variety of formats available can cause legibility problems when slides are viewed in different instructional locations.
- Economical slide duplication usually requires about ten working days for delivery, depending on local facilities. Faster service is available, but always with substantial extra charges.
- Artwork format must be specially designed for slides to be used with video.

Check List of Considerations for Selecting and Developing Slides for Instruction

Instructions. The following check list is intended to be used *after* the decision to use slides for visuals has been made. The list is intended as a mind-jogger to help you plan the production of the visuals for your project.

Group A is a series of questions designed to help you reevaluate your decision to use slides. Groups B, C, and D are to assist in planning the visual content of the instruction. Groups E and F are to help in the ordering and organization of slide materials.

A. Analyze lesson content to determine what visuals are needed, if any. All answers should be YES. A NO answer indicates you should reconsider your choice of medium. These questions pertain to slides used either as an instructional aid or an instructional medium.

	YES	NO
If the lesson is about objects or things that are unfamiliar to the student:		
Is it *impractical* to show the students the real thing due to size, cost, or safety reasons?	_____	_____
Is it easier to display visual representations of the objects or things that tell them about it?	_____	_____
Will still-visual displays satisfy learning needs? (Caution: Think over carefully. We often assume motion is critical when it is not).	_____	_____
Are there parts of the verbal message that can best be displayed visually? Such might include a description of an event or a situation where "one picture is worth a thousand words," or: parts of the verbal message that need to be stressed or repeated visually to enhance communication.	_____	_____
Is the verbal message sufficiently long or complex so that visuals *may* help keep student attention and help them follow the logic or purpose of the presentation?	_____	_____
If slides are used as an instructional aid only:		
Is it feasible to dim room lights for viewing?	_____	_____
Is it desirable for the instructor to have a locked-in (exact) format?	_____	_____

B. Describe the visuals needed on 3″ by 5″ or 5″ by 7″ storyboard cards, either in longhand description or by a rough pencil sketch.* If working with a script for narration, write the ideas for the script on the storyboard cards. To verify your planning for the visual display, complete the following checklist. All answers should be YES.

	YES	NO
Have you lean programmed your visuals to minimize both production cost and student distraction? (See "Developmental Testing.")	____	____
Have you checked local art or slide files for ideas or materials you can use without new production work?	____	____
If you need drawings or cartoons, have you checked available clip-art files?	____	____
Have you reviewed the section, "Rules of Thumb for Visuals"?	____	____

C. Review the storyboard visuals and the lesson content to see if materials should be resequenced to best utilize visual displays. If student or instructor is to work with various media, plan transitions smoothly to reduce distraction.

D. Edit visuals in hand-drawn form and combine them with slides already available for the lesson. Check the following items. All answers should be YES.

	YES	NO
If dealing with objects or things, have you considered whether the students are familiar with them?	____	____
If students are *not* familiar with the objects or things, did you provide visuals to show perspective, early in the lesson, regarding size, shape and, relationships of parts?	____	____
If displaying tools or equipment with which the students will be working on the job, did you show them an over-the-shoulder view as they will actually see and work with them on the job?	____	____
Did you use a horizontal format?	____	____
Are the graphics that are planned simple and clear?	____	____
Did you consider visual legibility? (See the legibility formulas in "Rules of Thumb for Visuals."	____	____
Did you avoid busy, distracting visuals?	____	____

*Suggestions on storyboarding techniques are included in, *Planning and Producing Audio Visual Materials*, by J. Kemp. See "Selected References."

Are all the visuals necessary?   ____ ____

Have you checked your visuals with an expert on the subject matter to ensure accuracy?   ____ ____

E. Order visuals from your institutional studio laboratory or photographic supply house. Check to be sure the following information is specified on the original order. All answers should be YES.

YES   NO

Are slides to be duplicated from existing masters rather than other duplicates?   ____ ____

If slides are to be made from existing clip-art or other readily available materials, was it noted on the order?   ____ ____

Were local arrangements made for slides to be shot on location?   ____ ____

Is the horizontal format stipulated on the order?   ____ ____

Did you plan for sufficient lead time for slides requiring original artwork? (Preparation of artwork requires a longer production time and will be handled individually.) Again specify horizontal format.   ____ ____

Have you arranged to maintain contact with the supplier to resolve problems arising in legibility, cost, or redesign of lesson materials?   ____ ____

F. After receiving slide materials, complete the following checklist. All answers should be YES.

YES   NO

Do all visuals meet the 6W formula for legibility? (See "Rules of Thumb for Visuals.")   ____ ____

Have you reviewed, sequenced, and numbered the master set of slides? (See suggestions for organization and storage on the next page.)   ____ ____

Has a subject matter expert checked the visuals for accuracy?   ____ ____

Have you maintained a horizontal format?   ____ ____

Have you filed the original slides with all essential data, including the name of the course, for storage as the master for duplication? (See suggestions in the following section.)   ____ ____

Suggestions for Organizing and Storing Slides

In order to set up, sequence, and number master copies of slides, always start with a *black* slide as number 1. To number slides for viewing:

Set up slides on lighted viewer, arranged in lesson sequence.

Place a small dot in the lower left-hand corner of the slide as viewed correctly. (See Fig. A.)

Turn slide upside down—the dot will be in upper right-hand corner—and write the slide number to the left of the dot as shown in Fig. B.

When assembling the slides in the tray, the number on the slide should be in the upper *right*-hand corner, over the number on the slide tray base.

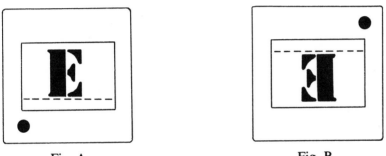

Fig. A   Fig. B

Store master copies of slides in a safe, cool place. To avoid handling lesson slides, store them in the slide tray or carousel in which they will be used.

Use slides mounted in plastic or glass in 80-slide trays only. Use of 140-slide trays is not encouraged because slides often jam in the projector.

Project on a proper sized screen to ensure legibility. Remember, the 6W formula requires 1 foot of screen width for each 6 feet of viewing distance from the screen.

When ordering duplicate slide copies of slide *sets* to be made, specify in your order whether you want the duplicates collated and numbered.

If word slides are requested, avoid water-colored Kodalith slides when many duplicate copies will be necessary.

If Super Slides must be duplicated, they can generally be ordered less expensively in 31mm.

FILMSTRIPS

Filmstrips, like slides, provide a projected visual image that can be used as an instructional aid or, when combined with an audio device or printed material, as an instructional medium. In fact there are many similarities between these two media in production and application. The principle differences between filmstrips and slides are in the mode of packaging and in the equipment for utilization. Both are made with 35mm motion picture type film; filmstrips, however, use the film in continuous strips with each visual composed in a single, horizontal frame. This technique of using the format of 35mm motion picture film provides one of the advantages of filmstrips, because continuous processing in high-speed printing and developing equipment makes duplication of multiple copies economical and rapid. Another advantage of filmstrips in comparison with slides, which must be packaged individually, is that filmstrips provide many pictures on one field of film that is light in weight and requires little storage space.

The choice between using either slides or filmstrips for visuals is primarily dependent, therefore, on the utilization and delivery system adopted and the number of duplicates needed for distribution. However, with the increasing use of individualized instruction, and more frequent situations requiring long course life and distribution of program packages to large student populations, there is a markedly increased use of filmstrips throughout educational and training institutions.

Relating Filmstrips to Instructional Objectives

Class of media: Instructional aid *or* instructional medium (when used in conjunction with audio or print).

Characteristics: Still visual.

Application to type of learning:

Cognitive objectives. Filmstrips can be used to teach recognition and/or discrimination of relevant visual stimuli; for example, they can:

Teach recognition of unfamiliar objectives or things displaying visual representations, pictures, or drawings.

Teach discrimination skills by contrasting objects shown at the same time or sequentially.

Enhance teaching of discrimination skills by means of line drawings that exaggerate differences in objects.

Present representations of working locations, positions, or situations that students will face in typical job environments.

They can also be used to teach rules, principles, and sequences of events; for example, they can:

Explain principles of objects by showing internal working parts using cut-away views.

Reinforce and clarify the instructor's narrative through the use of visual representations such as charts, diagrams, and scales.

Display verbally, by words or statements, points to be stressed in the instructor's narration.

Clarify and reinforce instruction given orally by also displaying statements about the lesson content and purposes.

Psychomotor objectives. Little, if any application. Still-visual displays can point out positions of moving items, ways to hold items to be manipulated, or critical points in the movement of objects. Artwork can suggest direction and intensity of motion.

Affective objectives. Not really applicable. Even when well done and combined with audio taped materials, the filmstrip medium is similar to slide and tape presentations, and does not have the impact of either video or motion film for influencing attitudes.

Advantages and Disadvantages of Filmstrips

Advantages. Filmstrips can be used as either an instructional aid *or* an instructional medium. As an instructional aid, filmstrips permit instructors to:

- Control the pace of the presentation.
- Back up visual displays to review specific points.
- Capitalize on a large visual display to point out critical items.

As an instructional medium (when used in combination with audio or print), filmstrips provide locked-in visual content and sequence, which ensures both lesson integrity, and against visuals being lost, reversed, or out of sequence. The compact size of visuals accommodates the production and distribution of individualized lesson material. Inherent advantages of filmstrips are:

- They are easily reproducible in large quantities.
- They can be used with both front and rear-screen projection.
- They are small, which permits compact packaging and storing, ease of distribution, and convenient transportation for use in various locations.
- Reproduction of filmstrips in large quantities is generally more economical than slides in cost per projected visual.
- Packaging problems are minimal. Standard containers for filmstrips, with or without audio components, are available to make lesson units easy to store, distribute, and use.
- Since filmstrips with sound are packaged with audio accompaniment on discs, tapes, or (usually) cassettes, alternative sound tracks for different audiences are easily provided, such as in various foreign languages or for technical and nontechnical audiences.
- Versatility of display design allows for progressive disclosure of information, the suggestion of motion, and special effects through photography and/or artwork and graphics.
- Equipment for projecting and viewing filmstrips, with or without sound, is available in a wide variety of types and costs. Modern machines are compact, easy to use, generally reliable, and easily transported.

Disadvantages.

- Filmstrips generally require dimmed lighting for adequate visual display; they require room darkening and light control when used as an instructional aid.
- Because of the locked-in sequence of visuals on a strip of 35mm film, editing and updating of filmstrip materials may become more time consuming and expensive than slides.
- Since several modes of providing sound for use with filmstrips are available, it is essential for course developers to determine what kind of equipment is necessary for utilizing programs to be produced, and to select the proper audio medium (disc, tape, or cassette) and synchronization method.
- Artwork for filmstrips and photographs on 2 × 2 slides to be used in filmstrips require a 3:4 ratio of height to width. See the sketch below

showing the area of a 2 × 2 slide for a filmstrip format indicated by the vertical broken lines.

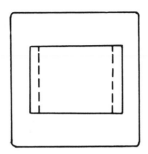

• Because filmstrip processing requires copy stand and laboratory processing, the time required for the preparation of release prints is often longer than processing slides.

Check List of Considerations for Selecting and Developing Filmstrips for Instruction

Instructions. Segment A lists a series of questions designed to help you confirm or reevaluate your decision to use filmstrips as a visual medium. The remaining questions in sections B and C are intended to help plan the development of your lesson material and guide you in your contacts with production personnel.

A.   Analyze lesson content and objectives to determine if this medium is best suited to your needs. All answers should be YES.

	YES	*NO*
Is it desirable for the visual display to be locked-in, prohibiting resequencing or editing of visual content?	___	___
Is the lesson content stable, requiring little updating or editing in the near future?	___	___
Is the lesson content primarily visual, or does it require visual support?	___	___

For further confirmation that filmstrips are a desirable choice, a YES answer is required for at least one of the following criteria:

Is the message about objects or things with which the students are unfamiliar?	___	___
Is it easier to show students *representations* of objects or things than the real things?	___	___
Are there parts of the verbal message that *must* be emphasized by visual reinforcement or through progressive build-up of visualized ideas?	___	___
Is the audio message sufficiently long so that visuals will help keep student attention and interest?	___	___
Is it necessary for the visual message to be *exactly* the same in both content and sequence for each presentation?	___	___
Will it be necessary to duplicate and ship many copies of the lesson, which includes visuals?	___	___
If lesson is instructor centered, is it feasible to dim the room lights?	___	___

B. Considering your course objectives and lesson content, prepare a list in sequence of visuals that are necessary. All answers below, when applicable, should be YES.

	YES	NO
If dealings with objects or things with which the students are unfamiliar:		
Have you planned to give the students, early in the lesson, views of objects in relation to things with which they are familiar to help them discriminate about the size and shape?	____	____
Have you planned to show over-the-shoulder views of the things during the lesson? (How they will see the things on the job.)	____	____
If objects or things have internal working parts that are essential to the lesson, have you planned for cut-away, sectioned, or enlarged views?	____	____
If you plan to use visual representations of things, do they represent real-world conditions, such as:		
Can work locations and conditions be displayed realistically?	____	____
Will safety requirements and local work policies be displayed correctly?	____	____
If presenting a verbal message that can best be described visually, have you planned visuals to be as simple as possible to avoid student confusion or distraction?	____	____
If verbal messages are to be supported by visuals:		
Have you avoided excessive numbers of visuals to reduce distraction?	____	____
Have points to be stressed been treated with visual techniques, including progressive build-up or disclosure, and by visual repetition of important points when desirable?	____	____

C. As you plan development and production of lesson visuals, check the following:

	YES	NO
Have you reviewed the "Guidelines for Visuals" to remind yourself of possible problem areas, such as legibility and formats?	____	____
Have you reviewed the "Developmental Testing" section?	____	____
Have you discussed your filmstrip production requirements with your in-house or available outside commercial producers to be sure they can meet your needs?	____	____
Have you arranged for a subject matter expert to check the accuracy of all visuals (and script, if sound is to be used)?	____	____

6 _____Motion Visuals

FILM AND VIDEO

Unfortunately, course writers and developers can be misled by those who hold firm convictions for or against either film or television for instructional purposes. After a number of years in which these two media have been treated as competitive and unique systems, experiences in the production of motion pictures for entertainment, news, and education have resulted in a blending: TV and film are clearly becoming interlocked as coordinate systems. Finished productions are made from undercutting of film and video; productions are made on video systems and transferred to film for distribution; production techniques in both media are becoming less distinctive, and effects and treatment of content peculiar to each are seldom identified by any but the most experienced observers. From the viewpoint of the user, the student is simply being taught or informed by motion visuals.

It is possible to make long lists of likenesses and differences between film and television. However, to accommodate the average course developer's responsibilities, the following material is focused upon those comparisons, advantages, and disadvantages that relate directly to the problems of selection and development of motion visuals for the purposes of communicating instructional content. This will, of course, involve some issues such as distribution plans. Still, the more technical differences between film and video, which are not relevant to your problems of planning for production, distribution, and utilization, you can with comfort, leave to the engineers and craft specialists.

One important factor in the selection of video productions of many organizations is the availability of in-house facilities to produce motion visuals. Possibly due to this factor alone, institutional films tend to be produced through commercial studios. Because of this situation, more emphasis will be placed in the video section; however, most of the developmental steps suggested in the check lists will be the same for film as for video.

Some Rules of Thumb for Producing Motion Visuals

Whether working with video or film, here are some rule-of-thumb guides to keep in mind when considering motion visuals for production:

- These media are primarily designed to show motion *not* still pictures.
- Motion visuals are excellent for affective (attitude-changing) presentations.
- For instructional purposes motion visuals are best used on a one-to-one relationship. Regardless of audience size, scripts should be aimed at a student as an individual.
- The sound track *must* be relevant to the visuals and should be in the *active* voice.
- The narration should *not* tell what is happening on the screen, unless interpretation or clarification is necessary, *or* a critical point must be stressed.
- All motion visual media have an *exact content* and should be edited and validated before presentation. *Before* releasing, check the materials with a subject matter expert and also with small, representative groups of students.
- Since both video and motion film are essentially visual media, the narration should be developed on the basis of a carefully designed visual script. The writer must think in visuals.
- Remember, you don't really have a captive audience; the audience can mentally turn you off. Your script plan must include consideration of the attitudes of the viewers.

• Production of motion visual materials is a complex operation, requiring the participation of people from varied disciplines and technical skills. Functioning by approval of a committee only adds to expense, frustration, and confusion. The responsibility for approval at various stages of production and for the acceptance of the final product should rest with one person. Whoever has that final responsibility should be designated as the producer and be available for coordinating with the various production groups.

These rules are not by any means a comprehensive statement of all the pitfalls or the benefits of motion visual media. They may not even be applicable in every case. This section is not intended to help perpetuate the controversy of film versus video when considered as competitive media. Motion picture film and video each have characteristics that make it the writer's most practical choice based on circumstances and individual need, considering the advantages and disadvantages outlined in the following material.

The guidelines and check lists for each of these media are simply intended to provide you with a basic and organized approach to the pre-production stages of instruction using motion visual media to help increase the likelihood of a successful product.

Video Related To Instructional Objectives

Class of media: Instructional medium.

Characteristics: Motion visual, audio or silent.

Application to types of learning:

Cognitive objectives. Video can:

Be used to teach recognition and/or discrimination of relevant motion stimuli, such as: Relative speed of moving objects, deviations in movement, and interactions of objects and things; it is possible (but not often economical) to display a series of relevant *still* visuals with or without audio stimuli, as would be done with slides, photographs, and audio recorders.

Be used to teach rules and principles; it is possible (but not economical) to display series of words (verbal abstractions) as with other still visuals or print.

Be particularly useful to provide *immediate* feedback to students concerning their performance, as they display their skills and their ability to apply rules and principles.

Psychomotor objectives. Video is:

Useful to model motion skills. It can exaggerate motion (slow or fast) to teach mind-body coordinations, such as techniques in manipulating tools, climbing, or swimming.

Useful to provide immediate visual feedback to students on their ability to perform motion skills.

Affective objectives. Video is very useful for creating attitudes and emotions by the use of various techniques and effects. It is an excellent tool for displaying affective information.

Advantages and Disadvantages of Video

Advantages. With video you can:

- Reproduce motion (with or without sound) to display both relevant stimuli and desired student responses required by the instruction. One example of this use is displaying vignettes that show the interaction of people, to show the student what should (or should not) be done.

- Provide instant replay to critique or evaluate the performance of: students, by taping selected actions for use in courses on how to develop interpersonal skills, for example; interviewing techniques, conducting meetings, and giving presentations; and instructors or speakers, for guidance in editing material before final presentation.

- Produce visual effects to enhance either the learning process or entertainment value of the presentation. Depending on the writer's intent and ability to visualize effects (and the production staff); some of the effects that can be produced on video tape are: compression or extension of time or illusion of activities going on at the same time; split or multiple screen images for a variety of visual cues; a smooth flow of visual changes from one scene to the next; and the exaggeration of motion through various speeds from slow to fast.

- Lock in content and sequencing of the training used interactively with workbooks, guides, texts, tools, or other things used on the job.

- Produce the same information simultaneously to various sized audiences in different locations by having monitors in various classrooms.

Disadvantages.

- Implementing materials requires video equipment to be locally available and compatible with the video tape (on reel or in cassette) that is distributed.

- Video script writing is difficult and time consuming.

- Production costs are high, and talented production teams scarce.

- Visual quality when transferred to film may be poor.

- Small monitor screens limit audience size unless multiple monitors or video projection systems are used.

- The amount of lettering on graphics for video is limited to about one-half that of film or still visuals.

- Care must be taken when using colored graphics for black and white TV. For example; some shades of red and green appear the same on a black and white screen. If working with black and white video; whenever possible use graphics made in black and white and shades of gray.

- Rapid changes in technology make obsolescence of video systems a continuing problem.

Check List of Considerations for Selecting and Developing Video for Instruction

Preparing video training materials is both expensive and complex. To anticipate all the problems and contingencies the course writer should be aware of during this process would be impossible. These guidelines, therefore, do *not* represent an all-inclusive list of considerations that will guarantee success. What is presented here is a set of mind-joggers to be used in conjunction with some suggested production guidelines located at the end of this section. Segment A is to help you reconsider your choice of medium while segments B through M are to help in the planning and development of materials.

A. Reevaluate your media selection:

Analyze lesson objectives, content, and distribution considerations to determine if *video* is the best choice of medium. All answers should be YES.

	YES	*NO*
Is motion critical to the lesson? (Caution: We often assume motion is critical when it is *not*. To answer yes to this question, *at least* one of the following criteria should apply to your lesson content:)	____	____

It is necessary to display motion in an exaggerated form.

Motion is *necessary* to demonstrate psychomotor skills required to manipulate objects or perform physical activities.

Motion is *necessary* to display changing visual cues used by people interacting with each other, e.g., changes in facial expression and body movement associated with verbal communications.

Motion is *necessary* to display special effects or to develop an emotion or an attitude because the lesson content is primarily affective.

Immediate visual feedback is necessary to display students' physical and verbal performance.

Is a locked-in content and sequence desirable?	____	____
Does the lesson require exact reproduction?	____	____
Will the lesson be displayed to small groups (rather than large audiences), and is video equipment available for display?	____	____
Does the life of the course (or some other factor) justify the expense of video?	____	____

B. Briefly outline the lesson content into a logical order of presentation. Review the "Rules of Thumb for Visuals," as well as suggestions in "Developmental Testing."

C. Prepare a storyboard outline for visual presentation in either rough sketch or verbal form. Check the following items: (All answers should be YES.)

	YES	NO
Have you reviewed the section on developmental testing?	___	___
Are visual scenes simple and direct?	___	___
Have you planned to give the students perspective regarding the size and shape of objects or things with which they are unfamiliar?	___	___
Will students see tools, equipment, or work locations as they will see them on the job?	___	___
Have you avoided displaying a series of still visuals that could be shown less expensively by another medium?	___	___

D. Review the planned visuals and rough narrative with a subject matter expert. All answers to the following should be YES.

	YES	NO
Does the sequence of events displayed match the real job?	___	___
Are accurate working conditions, practices, and rules followed in the visuals?	___	___
Does the narrative portion describe the job accurately?	___	___

E. Rough draft the visual scenes down the left-hand side of note paper, then fill in the supporting narrative alongside the visual portion. A suggested script format for video materials is shown at the end of this section.

F. Revise the rough draft of the script until you are satisfied with this *initial* draft. Check the following. All answers should be YES.

	YES	NO
Have you kept the narrative lean? (Video is primarily a visual medium.)	___	___
Have you avoided repeating verbally what is shown on the screen?	___	___
Have you used colloquial speech and avoided jargon and technical terms when possible? (See suggestions for audio scripts written to support visuals in "Audio" to guide you in evaluating the audio portion of your script.)	___	___

Have you avoided expensive location shots when possible?   ____ ____

Have you avoided using only a talking face?   ____ ____

Have you planned the lesson to be directed toward one student rather than a large audience? (Television is best displayed on a one-to-one basis.)   ____ ____

Have you used the active voice in the audio portion of the script?   ____ ____

Have you avoided using long series of still visuals?   ____ ____

G. Review the section "Video Graphics," at the end of this section, then revise the initial script again to add visual and sound directions for the script, noting special effects and graphic requirements.

H. Edit initial script again. Note all directions, such as visuals, camera shots, and special effects. Consider the following. All answers should be YES.

	YES	NO
Have you avoided the talking face or excessive still visuals supported by narration?	____	____
Does your script have an opening, a body, and a closing?	____	____
If displaying someone doing something, have you planned to edit the activity so that you don't have one camera showing the entire scene? (Watching an event on the screen seems *much* longer than seeing it in real life.)	____	____
Have you considered what special effects will be needed to enhance and clarify the presentation, and have you made note of them in the script?	____	____

I. Have script typed double spaced as shown in the video script sample at the end of the section. Edit again, if necessary, to ensure that: the visual display has continuity and is accurate; the audio narration supports the visuals and is written to be heard—not read! When video is used interactively with workbooks, the students are directed to workbook or worksheet pages by the video display, and back to the video by the print.

J. Review script with a subject matter expert to ensure accuracy of content and credibility with target population. Edit where necessary.

K. Complete the developmental testing of the material with representative students until you are satisfied that the instruction and media work.

L. Complete the Preproduction notes for use by local production groups. (See suggested model at the end of this section.)

M. Arrange with local or outside video production personnel for taping. (A suggested request form is included at the end of this section.)

Video Graphics

Review the section "Rules of Thumb for Visuals" in this book for assistance in planning the legibility and format of video graphics.

Illustrations for use in video productions may include: photographs, slides, transparencies, motion pictures, graphics, poster boards, chalkboard displays, and easel and flip chart displays.

The TV format ratio is 3:4. Use artwork proportions compatible with this ratio, for example: 6×8, 9×12, 12×16.

Allow for a loss of margin in artwork and slides due to variations in adjustment of television receivers.

When using 35mm slides for TV, use a horizontal format, and compensate for the ratio difference by allowing extra margin on each side of the viewing area.

Because the video legibility formula is 12W, it is necessary that graphics be bold and free from unnecessary details, and that printed outlines or lists must be limited to: no more than 5–7 lines; no more than 3–5 words per line; and that visuals be legibility "proofed" as described in "Rules of Thumb for Visuals."

Motion picture film may reproduce satisfactorily on video tape. Film clips may be available from which portions can be used to improve the quality of the program lesson. Be careful not to break copyright laws; be sure you have the right to copy.

Avoid graphics of questionable visual quality. When possible use the original or master copy.

FILM

The course developer who chooses to work in this medium is faced with a dilemma. On the one hand it is often not profitable to do so cheap a production that the students may turn the message off. On the other hand, as stated in the 1973 Ford Foundation study: "To use the CTW (Sesame Street) organization to produce a ten minute program on the breeding of fruit flies is like using a cannon to kill a mouse."

Once the decision to use film as an instructional medium has been reached, however, consideration *must* be given to the problems of: availability of production and display facilities; preproduction plans; and expense approval. These issues must be resolved early in the lesson development.

Because of the many similarities between film and video, there will necessarily be some overlap in characteristics, advantages, and disadvantages. Nevertheless, some differences, primarily in distribution, display characteristics, and processing time do exist and *must* be considered by course developers. These differences will be pointed out below.

Film Related to Instructional Objectives

Class of media: Instructional medium.

Characteristics: Motion visual (audio or silent).

Application to types of learning:

Cognitive objectives. Film can be used to:

Teach recognition and/or discrimination of relevant motion stimuli, e.g., speed of moving objects, deviations in movement, etc. It is possible (but not economical) to display series of relevant *still* visuals with audio stimuli as would be done with slides or filmstrips and audio recorders.

Teach rules, principles, etc. It is possible (but not economical) to display series of words (verbal abstractions) as with other still visuals or print.

Psychomotor objectives. Film is used to model motion skills. It can exaggerate motion (slow or fast) to teach mind–body coordination, e.g., techniques in manipulating tools, climbing, swimming, etc. It is also useful to provide delayed visual feedback to students on their ability to perform motion skills.

Affective objectives. Film is most useful to create attitudes and emotions by the use of various techniques and effects. It is an excellent tool for displaying affective information through the use of optical effects and associated visual imagery.

Advantages and Disadvantages of Film

Advantages. Film has advantageous characteristics as listed below.

• It enables reproduction of color or black and white visuals with motion to display relevant stimuli or responses required in training.

• Special visual effects can be produced that may enhance learning. These effects are particularly helpful in presenting affective materials and can increase student involvement. Depending on the writer's creativity and imagination, *some* film effects are: compression or extension of time or the illusion of activities going on at the same time; split or multiple images on one screen or a variety of visual distortions and illusions; a smooth flow of visual changes from one scene to the next; and the exaggeration of motion through slow, stop, or fast speeds.

- The variety of available film sizes and types can provide visual displays for use with large audiences (unlike video) and small groups or for individual viewing.
- Film (unlike video) can be used with both front and rear screen projection.
- The content and sequencing of training materials can be locked-in and also used interactively with workbooks, lesson guides, etc.
- Film projectors are generally more readily available than video equipment (even in remote locations), portable, and simple to operate.
- The quality of visual and sound, when transferred to video tape is generally better than transfer of video to film.

Disadvantages. Note these drawbacks:

- Production costs are high and talented production teams are scarce.
- Film processing requires time for development. There are no instant feedback capabilities.
- Institutions frequently do not have low-cost, in-house facilities for producing quality sound films.
- Film stock cannot be erased and reused.
- Care must be taken in the handling of films to prevent breakage; films must be cleaned regularly.

Checklist of Considerations for Selecting and Developing Film for Instruction

Because of the many similarities in the development processes required for film and video, the following information is brief and the video check list should be used for development purposes. The following points, however, should be kept in mind when preparing instruction on motion film.

When reconsidering your choice of media in step A of the video check list, keep in mind that: film is used *primarily* for viewing by large audiences; in-house film production and editing facilities may be limited; and initial production costs for film may be higher than video.

When reviewing the "Rules of Thumb for Visuals," remember that: film graphics are based on the 6W formula; film format is a horizontal 3 to 4 ratio; and duplicate copies should be ordered from the original internegative.

You should consult your local production personnel about your plans as early as possible.

Some suggested formats for scripting and production requests are included at the end of this section. The formats are designed to be used for either video or film.

Sample Script

Location: Local Office

Scene I

VISUAL	*NARRATION*
Title: Step 1 Preparation (2sec)	
Fade to: Bert writing letter at desk. (Establishing LS of office) Art walks up and leans over.	ART: HEY BERT/GOT A PROBLEM/ COULD I SEE YOU?
(MS working in as close as possible.)	BERT: SURE ART/WHAT'S THE PROBLEM?
	ART: CHUCK LEWIS PULLED THE 8:30 TO 5:30 SHIFT AND WALLY GOT THE 8 TO 5 ALL NEXT WEEK.
Bert: Quizzical look.	BERT: THAT'S RIGHT/DID CHUCK COME TO SEE YOU?
	ART: UH HUH/YOU *KNOW* WALLY HAS LESS SENIORITY.
	BERT: YES, BUT LET ME CHECK THE SCHEDULE AND WE CAN GET TOGETHER ON THIS LATER THIS AFTERNOON/SAY RIGHT AFTER LUNCH.
Bert turns to clerk on pause.	BERT: JUST A SECOND//JANE/IS THE CONFERENCE ROOM AVAILABLE THIS AFTERNOON?
Cut to Jane. Jane picks up schedule, looks through to page.	JANE: JUST A / YES/FREE ALL AFTERNOON.
	BERT: *GOOD*/I'LL BE IN THERE WITH ART/LET'S MEET THERE AFTER LUNCH/I'LL BRING THE NEW SCHEDULE AND THE PREVIOUS ONE TOO/O.K.?
On pause, Bert turns to Art. Art smiles, turns and leaves. Bert gets out schedules and copy of contract.	
(Zoom to CU)	ART: OK/SEE YOU THERE.

Sample of Preproduction Notes: Union Grievance Procedure

SETTING:

Narrator sitting at (or on) desk. Easel sheets slightly off stage. Union contract book for narrator to hold.

Vignettes shot in studio. Props require two office desks for office scenes; one table and setting of chairs for conference room scene. Door visible in both scenes.

SPECIAL EFFECTS:

Superimposed graphics (35mm word slides).

One split screen.

Fades between scenes.

Filtered voice on "thinking" shot.

Filtered voice on phone.

LOCATION:

All scenes should be shot in studio with sufficient quality to provide optical transfer to 16mm at a future date.

TALENT:

Professional talent narrator (male) with good presence and relaxed manner. Bert and Art *may* be professional with Art being a younger man. Manager and clerk can be of local talent.

COSTUMES:

Bert should be wearing sports jacket and tie, Art in shirt sleeves (no tie). Manager (Wally) in suit and tie. No make-up.

SHOOTING SEQUENCE:

Suggest narrators' scenes be shot at one time. Vignette scenes edited in later.

Suggest the two vignettes be shot at same time with fades between each scene. For rerun of the "good" vignette, fades can be shortened to provide visual continuity.

Sample Production Request

Video _____   Film _____   Date _____

Production Format   Producer/Writer: _____

Tape size _____   _____

Open reel _____   Cassette _____   _____

Film size _____   Company: _____

Internegative   *Yes* _____   No _____   _____

                                              Program Title: _____

                                              _____

                                              Deadline—When must master be ready?

                                              _____

TARGET AUDIENCE: Who is the program intended for? _____
_____
_____

TALENT: Who will arrange for talent personnel? Writer _____

                                  Production Group _____

What talent will be used? Professional _____

                 Nonprofessional _____

Name(s) and Telephone Number(s) of local talent used: _____
_____
_____
_____
_____
_____
_____

Are preproduction notes completed and attached?   Yes _____   No _____

Are, at least, three copies of script attached?   Yes _____   No _____

List visuals needed for production: (include title and logo if used).

1. _____   6. _____

2. _____   7. _____

3. _____   8. _____

4. _____   9. _____

5. _____   10. _____

Note type of visual needed, slides, chart, easel, etc. (*Show additional visuals on reverse side of this form.*)

APPROVAL: Name of person who has authority to approve expenditures and accept product: _____

DISTRIBUTION: How many copies will be required? _____

FORMAT NEEDED: Tape: Reel _____   Size _____

   Cassette _____   Size _____

Film: Reel _____   Size _____

   Cassette _____   Size _____

Sample List of Personnel

The list below is an example of *some* of the personnel a course developer *might* come in contact with when dealing with a large video or film studio. A brief description of each staff member's responsibilities is included as general information. In a small in-house production group, the staff is obviously smaller, and several responsibilities or functions may be assumed by one person.

Title	Responsibility
Producer	Responsible for creation and production of a single show. Passes approval during various stages of production and accepts final responsibility for the end product.
Production Assistant	Handles such details as clearing music rights, delivery of graphics, etc.
Unit Manager	Acts as business manager in seeing that costs are kept within production budget.
Director	Determines the creative aspects of the show and directs the camera during taping.
Assistant Director	Responsible for the timing of the show, cues in special effects and music, and prepares camera shots.
Floor or Stage Manager	Directs the activities on the floor of the studio, and cues performers and stage hands.
Technical Director	In charge of all technical personnel and runs the console during taping.
Audio (or Sound) Director	Responsible for all audio in the production.
Video Director	Handles master video recorder during the production.

7 Audio

AUDIO IN GENERAL

From the perspective of a course developer, audio materials provide an economical and convenient source of instructional content that can readily be made available for students. Once packaged, lesson content and sequence are exact—locked-in—and function as an instructional medium for independent study.

When appropriately prepared and well used, audio programming can be produced and distributed at a relatively low cost. When inappropriately designed and poorly used, audio programming can be an expensive disruption in student learning. Thus, as with any other medium, audio instruction must be done with skill and artistry, and with advance planning as carefully done as with any other medium.

Most course developers are accustomed to writing materials intended to be *read* by students. Writing habits are normally developed on a basis of rules that produce an acceptable literary style. After lesson content and sequence are established, the writer is concerned about the end product—print—and associated rules governing grammar, sentence structure, paragraphing, punctuation, conciseness, and spelling.

Techniques associated with writing lessons to be *heard*, however, require unique skills and have different measures of quality. Not that rules of good grammar and clear expression should be ignored in writing lines to be spoken, but to produce lines that can be spoken naturally and clearly—involves attention to such characteristics as:

Rhythm.

Combinations of words and sounds that can be articulated easily, clearly, and smoothly.

Structure that places key words in places where the listener can be sure to hear them. (For example, the first words spoken may not be heard with certainty, since the listener may need to focus his attention in order to receive important message words; thus, the sentence structure may begin with attention-getting words that lead up to a key word or statement.)

Sentence structures that are generally short and not complex. (That is, the ideas are packaged in complete statements, or in short phrases with clearly presented ideas.) Since a narration, unlike material that is read, marches along at a pace not controlled by the listener, the writer must be certain that the ideas presented are packaged for easy, quick, and accurate acquisition by the listener.

These sample characteristics indicate the complexity of the writer's job. Unfortunately, in this brief guide, only general suggestions can be given. You are urged to practice, read your own writing aloud into a recorder, listen, evaluate your work and, even more important, have others listen to your recording, and let their reactions help you improve your work.

These guidelines are *not* a panacea for all the woes of script writers. They simply present a systematic and time-tested approach used by professional writers to produce good audio material. The technical and procedural suggestions included in this material for recording master tapes and duplicate copies, is to ensure the best quality transmission to the student.

As with most specialized skills, the ability to write for the listener varies from individual to individual. For example, it may be difficult for some people to think visually and thereby prepare a lean, supporting script for a visual presentation. That skill deficiency, however, is *not* an excuse to give up or to select another, less appropriate medium. Assistance is usually available, and with time and patience adequate skills can be developed.

The audio medium can be used in several different ways: alone, or with printed materials, or in conjunction with slides or some other still visuals. Each use requires different techniques for developing the audio script. To accommodate this situation, this section will be divided into the following subsections: applications, advantages, and disadvantages of audio materials; script development for audio only (or audio used with printed materials), and review of the selection decision; script development for audio messages *supported* by still visuals; and script development for audio materials *supporting* still visual presentations.

Because *most* current instructional audio materials are produced in some kind of tape format, the check lists will deal only with that medium, rather than with scripts for live radio or telephone use; however, the same developmental techniques and procedures can be used for these and other types of audio media.

Relating Audio Material to Instructional Objectives

Class of media: Instructional medium.

Characteristics: Capable of presenting audio stimuli.

Application to types of learning:

Cognitive objectives.   Audio tapes can be used to teach recognition and/or discrimination of relevant audio stimuli. Some examples are:

To present the sound of a machine (or tool) with which students will be working, or sounds identifying malfunctions of the machine or tool to permit student discriminations among proper functions and malfunctions indicated by sounds.

To present the sound of specific alarms or other devices from which students should take action.

To teach recognition of dialects and accents associated with a job, or to present voices as they will sound on the job accompanied by shop noise or other interference, or customer voices on the telephone.

To present audio drills for learning to recognize foreign or unfamiliar words or phrases.

Audio can also teach rules and principles. When used for this purpose audio recordings usually are a substitute for, or are used in conjunction with printed matter, to add variety to the training or to ensure exact content.

Psychomotor objectives. Audio can be used to teach verbal skills, such as:

To permit the learner to hear and to imitate and practice the sounds of foreign or unfamiliar words.

To provide drills for the student to be able to recognize and practice sounds of words to overcome speech difficulties.

To give practice in making responses to spoken requests auditorially.

To present recorded drills in practicing to take orders or directions, with increasing rates of speed.

To present taped drills for practicing responses to alarms or signals, or other emergency audio communication or instructions.

Affective Objectives. Moods or attitudes may be established through use of background music, sound effects, and narrators' voices. Radio serial programs and advertisements (either live or taped) demonstrate these techniques.

Advantages and Disadvantages of Audio

Advantages:

- Lesson content is fixed—locked-in—and is exactly reproducible.
- Production and program reproduction are economical, and distribution is convenient.
- Equipment for utilizing audio programs is among the least costly of any of the audio-visual media.
- Through the use of various audio tape recording techniques, programmed instruction formats can be used for individualized instruction, allowing for self-pacing by the students, reinforcement, and immediate knowledge of performance.
- For sophisticated self-instructional program formats, devices are available to synchronize visuals with the recorded audio program, and provide automatic stop features to give students time to interact with the program and to proceed when ready. Other devices are especially designed for audio comparitor techniques, permitting students to hear a model performance, then to respond, and subsequently to compare their performance with the model.
- Moods or student attitudes can be affected through the use of background music and sound effects.

Disadvantages:

- Care must be exercised when using the audio channel alone for long periods without providing the student any visual stimulus. This can cause lessons to become boring and can inhibit self-paced instruction. (A 15 minute tape requires 15 minutes of student time, regardless of the student skills.)
- Revisions generally require a new master to be produced and new copies issued. This is time consuming and can result in considerable cost.
- Distribution problems can be encountered when producing synchronized visuals with audio tape due to the variety of hardware devices available and used in different training locations. Course developers must know what equipment is available to provide compatible software.
- Development of quality scripts (particularly those intended to support visuals) can be time consuming and require specialized skills.

- Caution must be exercised in pacing verbal content. Should material be presented to the student at too fast a speed, or should complex instructions be presented rapidly, the student may become lost or confused. It may be advisable in some cases to provide redundancy through visual reminders, e.g., restatements in workbook materials or displayed on still visuals. This can usually be determined during developmental testing.

- Student review of audio materials synchronized to still visuals can be difficult and confusing if the audio and visual materials get out of synchronization.

Check List of Considerations for Audio Only

The following check list is intended to be used as a mind-jogger when reviewing your media selection and developing lesson materials. Segment A is to help you reconsider this choice of media while segments B through G are to assist in planning, developing, and producing your instructional materials.

A. Review media selection. Consider lesson objectives and content; the audio medium must satisfy at least *one* of the following criteria:

	YES	NO
Are students unable to read, or do they have difficulty comprehending printed materials?	____	____
Does lesson material contain relevant audio stimuli to be presented to students? (See examples in the sample scripts at the end of this section.)	____	____
Does the lesson teach verbal skills or responses to verbal stimuli on the job?	____	____
Can audio be a practical way to add variety to instruction by changing media?	____	____

A Word of Caution:
Audio materials have a fixed time frame for presenting instruction. This implies that self pacing aspects of instruction and selection of content must be designed into the lesson materials.

B. *Prepare first draft.* Check script for the following criteria. All answers should be YES.

	YES	NO
Is the rough draft script either written or typed double-spaced, leaving a wide left-hand margin for notes?	____	____
Have you used language to be spoken, using a colloquial style normally used in conversational speech?	____	____
Have you used contractions whenever appropriate? We normally use such statements as: I'm, you're, haven't, and won't, rather than I am, you are, have not, and will not.	____	____
Have you eliminated big compound words? (The students don't care how smart you are and may not have a dictionary handy. Besides, you should make it as easy as possible for the narrator to speak clearly.)	____	____
Have you considered what sound effects and background noises may be necessary or desirable to establish realism or moods?	____	____

Have you avoided jargon and technical terms when possible? ____ ____

If you *had* to use some technical term did you spell the word phonetically in parenthesis so the narrator can pronounce it? ____ ____

Are the number of voices (characters) at a minimum for ease of production and to minimize cost? ____ ____

Have you had a subject matter expert check the lesson content to ensure relevance and accuracy? ____ ____

If script is to be used with printed (workbook) materials, have you:

Planned to present examples, when possible, to allow the student to practice interacting with the instructional materials? ____ ____

Compared the printed material with the script to be sure they are compatible? ____ ____

Planned to have the audio and printed material complement each other, e.g., tell the students on tape to turn to the printed material and referred them back to the audio portion in the workbook? ____ ____

C. *Tape first script on a cassette recorder.* Preferably someone other than the writer should record the script to help you be objective. As you listen to the tape check for: All answers should be YES.

	YES	NO
Was the script read exactly as written?	____	____
Were the messages clear?	____	____
Did the script sound natural, as if it were conversational and not being read?	____	____
Were there sufficient pauses built in to give the narrator time to breathe?	____	____
If there were any tongue-twisting phrases, did you revise them?	____	____
Did you remove unnecessary technical words or jargon when possible?	____	____
If the audio material is to be used with a student workbook (interactively), did you check the instructions to the student in both media to ensure they complement each other?	____	____

D. *Revise your first draft and then re-record on a cassette recorder.* Play back and check the following points. All answers should be YES.

	YES	NO
Was it read (preferably by someone other than the writer) exactly as written?	____	____
Does it meet the qualifications outlined for preparation of the first draft script?	____	____
Has the number of characters (or voices) been minimized for efficiency of recording?	____	____
Have necessary sound effects been noted? (Is it desirable to establish realism of location through such background sounds as office or street noises, and telephone voices and echoes?)	____	____

If the tape is to be used with a student workbook, have you:

	YES	NO
Emphasized brevity and clarity on the recorded instructions for the student?	____	____
Tested the audio product with the written material for ease of interaction?	____	____
Tested the length of the pauses to ensure sufficient time for the students to perform? Have you indicated how they will be told when to restart a stopped tape?	____	____
Have you checked the section, "Developmental Testing," for testing the material?	____	____

E. Developmentally test the material and revise the script again; then, if necessary, re-record and play back checking for the following criteria. All answers should be YES.

	YES	NO
Are words that need to be stressed, *underlined?*	____	____
Are pauses noted correctly and, when necessary, is the length of the pause stated in numbers of seconds?	____	____
Did you check to determine if music is necessary? (Avoid breaking copyright laws.)	____	____
Does a student or instructor have to adjust the volume?	____	____
Is it desirable, or possible, to set a mood through music (e.g., suspense, humor, period in time, etc.)?	____	____
Did you check to determine if any relevant audio stimuli were left out (e.g., sounds such as warning signals, shop noises, and engine or equipment sounds that are meaningful in the lesson)?	____	____
Did you have a subject matter expert check for the accuracy and realism of the audio presentation?	____	____

F. Write the final draft. Check typed copy as below. All answers should be YES.

                                          YES   *NO*

Is draft double-spaced and in the format shown in the samples at the end of this section?   _____ _____

Are sentences complete at the bottom of the page? (No sentence is carried over to the next page.)   _____ _____

Are words spelled correctly, so they will not be mispronounced? (Have you given directions for pronouncing unusual words?)   _____ _____

Are all pages numbered correctly?   _____ _____

Are words that need stress *underlined?*   _____ _____

Are instructions for the sound technician given at the beginning of the script? (These would include the sound effects required, music, and number and types of voices to be used. See the samples at the back of this section.)   _____ _____

G. Consult with production personnel for requirements for master tape, protection copies, and duplicates for release. See the suggestions at the end of the section.

                                          YES   *NO*

Have you determined in what format the audio programming will be released: cassettes or reels; how many copies will be ordered?   _____ _____

Have you allowed sufficient lead time for production and distribution?   _____ _____

Have you planned for packaging and labeling?   _____ _____

Have you prepared duplicate copies of script for use at the recording studio?   _____ _____

AUDIO SCRIPTS WITH VISUALS

The two basic types of cued audio scripts to be described in this section are: scripts using dialogue to support a visual message, and scripts using visuals to support a verbal message.

Preparing a visual message *supported* by narration or dialogue is more difficult to develop and is best compared with producing motion visuals. Many effective slide–tape or filmstrip presentations have been developed using this method, but for a writer to maintain a lean dialogue is a challenge because writers often have a tendency to write to be either heard or read, ignoring the primary message-carrying power of visuals.

Scripts using still visuals *to support* verbal content are more common and seemingly more natural for course writers to develop. Some examples of this method are narrated instructions using visuals as reference or to create a mood. In these cases, visuals are most commonly used as support to:

Occupy the audience's visual sense to keep its attention.

Clarify some verbal abstraction. ("One picture is worth a thousand words.")

Represent pictorially some object or thing about which the audience is unfamiliar. (See "Still Visuals.")

Elicit some emotional response from the audience.

Final script format. Regardless of the kind of program being written, when you use visuals in conjunction with audio materials, the final draft must follow the same format as shown in the samples that follow this section. The development process varies, however, and will be dealt with separately. The *important* fact is that the writer must determine *which* medium is carrying the principal message. Unless this is determined at the beginning of the project, the developer runs the risk of creating interference between the two media and inevitably impairing student learning.

Once the course developer has determined *which* channel (audio or visual), will be used principally to communicate the instructional content, the following check list sections can be used to develop the lesson script.

Check List for Scripts Using Visuals to Support an Audio Message

A. Prepare the first script following Steps B through D of the guidelines in the previous check list for audio only.

B. Read through the script and note these points where visuals may help support or are needed to clarify the lesson. Use the following check list:

	YES	NO
Is the audio message short, clear, and simple?	___	___
If your audio message is long or complex, will visuals help keep students' attention and/or clarify the verbal message? (If YES, identify places where either reinforcing or clarifying visuals will be used.)	___	___
Does your message deal with objects or things?	___	___

If YES, consider the following requirements:

	YES	NO
Are the students familiar with the objects or things in the lesson? (If your answer is NO, you *must* use visuals.)	___	___
When necessary, will a visual show the students items (size, color, and relationships) in comparison with something they know?	___	___
Will the visuals show students objects from the subjective viewpoint (as they will see the objects when they are working with them)?	___	___
Is it practical to show the students the real thing in the classroom? (If the answer is YES, you should use the real thing, and support the lesson, if needed, with still visuals.)	___	___

C. Prepare visuals for the lesson. (See the section on still visuals.)

	YES	NO
Have you checked the section, "Developmental Testing"?	___	___
Have you discussed your rough draft and rough visuals with a subject matter expert to ensure accuracy?	___	___

D. When rough visuals are complete, record the script on an audio cassette and play it back while viewing the rough visuals. Check the following points. All answers should be YES.

	YES	NO
Does the speech sound natural (conversational)?	___	___
Is the verbal message clear?	___	___
Are the visuals legible?	___	___

Are the visuals clearly and directly relevant to the narration? ____ ____

Have you avoided "cute," unrelated, or too elaborate visuals that may detract from the verbal message? ____ ____

Have you eliminated unnecessary narration or dialogue that could be replaced by visuals? ____ ____

Have you had a subject matter expert check the accuracy (or realism) of your message content and the correlation of voice and pictures? ____ ____

E. List the number of each visual down the left-hand column of the script giving a brief description or simple drawing of each. When using slides, start with slide number 1 as a black slide.

F. Developmentally test the materials until the lessons work and the students learn. (Check "Developmental Testing.")

G. Have final script typed according to the standard format at the end of this section. Check for the following characteristics. All answers should be YES.

	YES	NO
Is the script double-spaced and arranged in correct format?	____	____
Are all words to be stressed *underlined?*	____	____
Are sentences at the bottoms of pages complete (no sentence is carried to next page)?	____	____
Are all pages numbered correctly?	____	____
Are special instructions for music and sound effects given at the beginning of the script?	____	____
Are all cues marked properly?	____	____
Are all pauses indicated?	____	____

H. Have several duplicate copies made of the script for use by performers and production personnel, and order any necessary materials.

	YES	NO
Have you checked the production suggestions outlined at the end of this section?	____	____
Have you determined the format and how many copies of release tapes or cassettes will be ordered?	____	____
Have you allowed enough lead time for preparation of all materials?	____	____

Check List for Scripts Using Audio to Support a Visual Message

A. Outline the message content in rough form stating what you wish the student to see.

B. Prepare a rough storyboard of the lesson starting with visual notes or rough sketches. If you have not worked with the storyboard technique before, it might be wise to seek help at this stage.

C. Rough draft the script on the storyboard cards.*

D. Prepare a rough draft of the script. Check it for the following. All answers should be YES.

	YES	NO
Is the rough draft either written or typed double-spaced, leaving a wide left-hand margin for notes?	___	___
Have you used language to be spoken, using a colloquial style normally used in conversational speech?	___	___
Have you used contractions whenever appropriate? We normally use such statements as: I'm, you're, haven't, and won't, rather than I am, you are, have not, and will not.	___	___
Have you eliminated compound words? (The students don't care how smart you are and may not have a dictionary handy. Besides, you should make it as easy as possible for the narrator to speak clearly.)	___	___
Have you considered what sound effects and background noises may be necessary or desirable to establish realism or moods?	___	___
Have you avoided jargon and technical terms when possible?	___	___
If you *had* to use some technical term, did you spell the work phonetically in parentheses so the narrator can pronounce it?	___	___
Are the number of voices (characters) at a minimum for ease of production and to minimize cost?	___	___
Have you had a subject matter expert check the lesson content to ensure relevance and accuracy?	___	___

*A good description of working with storyboarding is given in *Planning and Producing Audio Visual Materials* by J. Kemp. See "Selected References."

E. Revise script as necessary and record it yourself or have someone else record it on a cassette recorder. Play it as you review the storyboard visuals. Check for the following. All answers should be YES.

	YES	NO
Will the visuals convey the intended message?	____	____
Does the narration or dialogue support and reinforce the messages in the visuals?	____	____
Does the narration discuss *only* what is in the visual and not wander to other topics or content?	____	____
Did you use conversational (colloquial) language?	____	____
Did you avoid big words, jargon, and technical terms when possible?	____	____
When you *had* to use technical terms, did you spell them phonetically (in parentheses) for the narrator?	____	____
Did you include music or sound effects when necessary?	____	____
Have you checked the script and planned visuals with a subject matter expert to ensure accuracy?	____	____

F. Review "Developmental Testing" section.

G. Produce the rough visuals and sequence the master set.

H. Developmentally test the material. (See "Developmental Testing.")

I. Edit the script and revise according to the results of testing. Retape the script yourself or have it renarrated by others exactly as written.

J. Play back the tape marking on the script words to be stressed and noting pauses. Check for the following. All answers should be YES.

	YES	NO
Have you checked materials again with a subject matter expert?	____	____
Are the visuals properly synchronized with the narration or dialogue?	____	____
Are the words to be stressed *underlined?* Are pauses indicated?	____	____
Were necessary sound effects and music noted?	____	____

K. Prepare the final draft by first checking the visuals and marking cues for change of visuals on the script. See the sample script at the end of this section. Before typing it, check the final draft for the following. All answers should be YES.

	YES	NO
Have you left a wide left-hand margin to add descriptions of visuals?	____	____
Did you finish sentences at the bottoms of pages (no sentences are carried over to the next page)?	____	____
Did you mark the cues with an asterisk or large dot for changes of visuals at the *ends* of sentences or, if a cue fell in the middle of a sentence, leave space for it to be noticed?	____	____
Are the pages numbered?	____	____
Are instructions included for sound effects, music, types of voices, and other production directions at the beginning of the script?	____	____

L. Number and briefly describe visuals in the left-hand column, to correspond with the script, as shown in the sample that follows on page 103.

M. Have the script typed. Check for the following. All answers should be YES.

	YES	NO
Is the final copy double-spaced?	____	____
Are cues marked with asterisks or large dots in the proper places (ends of sentences or wide space in middle of sentences)?	____	____
Are all pauses indicated and noted with time?	____	____
Is the format similar to the one used in the sample?	____	____

N. Have sufficient duplicate copies of script prepared and arrange for production of the master tape and duplicates with local production personnel.

	YES	NO
Have you reviewed the suggestions for producing master copies at the end of this section?	____	____
Have you determined the format and how many copies of the tapes are to be ordered?	____	____
Have you allowed sufficient lead time for production of both audio and visual materials?	____	____
Have you planned for packaging and labels?	____	____

Sample Script for Audio Only

Supervising Work Operations

Script Instructions: Miles' voice on phone filter throughout script. Sound effect: Telephone ring. (Two rings only)

Narrator: IF YOU HAVE ANSWERED TEST PROBLEM NUMBER 1 / YOU ARE READY TO LISTEN TO THE *FIRST* CONVERSATION ASSOCIATED WITH TEST PROBLEM NUMBER 2.

(telephone ringing)

Hillman: GARAGE / HILLMAN.

Miles: YEAH RAY / MILES // GOOD THING SWENSON'S WIFE CALLED IN *EARLY* TO SAY HE WOULDN'T BE IN / IT GAVE ME TIME TO GET RID OF HIS WORK LOAD *BEFORE* THE FELLAS LEAVE.

Hillman: RIGHT ROG / I'VE GOT MY LOAD SHEET HERE / WHAT ARE THE CHANGES?

Miles: FIRST // CANCEL LYNCH'S DAY OFF AND GIVE *HIM* ALL OF SWENSON'S MORNING WORK ORDERS.

Hillman: OK.

Miles: THEN GIVE THE *AFTERNOON* APPOINTMENTS TO JOHNSON.

Hillman: RIGHT.

Miles: THAT COVERS THE *REPAIR* ORDERS RAY / *I'LL* GIVE OUT THE *REST* OF THE ORDERS AS THE MEN ARE FREE.

Hillman: OK ROG / AFTER THE GUYS *LEAVE*, LEWIS AND I ARE GOING DOWN TO HILLWOOD // I'LL CALL YOU ABOUT TEN O'CLOCK?

Miles: TALK TO YOU LATER / SO LONG.

Narrator: NOW ANSWER THE QUESTION FOR TEST PROBLEM NUMBER 2. (pause 15 seconds) THE *NEXT* CONVERSATION YOU HEAR IS THE ONE FOR TEST PROBLEM NUMBER 3.

(telephone ringing—two rings)

Sample Script for Tape and Visuals

TITLE

PLANNING AND PROGRAMMING

Slides	*Voice*
1. Black slide (note: this slide is advanced before tape is started).	Music up 3 seconds—(Fade at slide 4 to voice over.)*
2. Title: THE "WHY" & "HOW" OF PLAN-PLANNING & PROGRAMMING.	/// * (4 seconds)
3. Company logo.	/// * (3 seconds)
4. Young girl on chair with a questioning look on face. (Music fades)	/// (3 seconds) *Narrator:* PLANNING IS DECIDING IN ADVANCE WHAT NEEDS TO BE DONE / AND*
5. Young boy holding sheet of paper entitled "WHEN."	*PROGRAMMING* IS THE SCHEDULING OF THOSE PLANS.*
6. Young girl asking, "WHY PLAN & PROGRAM?"	*Girl:* WELL / THAT SOUNDS GOOD // BUT IS IT *REALLY* ALL THAT NECESSARY? // MOST MANAGERS *KNOW* WHAT THEY HAVE TO DO // *WHY* SHOULD THEY WASTE THEIR VALUABLE TIME *PLANNING* THAT TIME // WHY NOT LET THEM GET ON WITH DOING ALL THE THINGS THEY HAVE TO DO?*
7. Story title: THE CASE OF THE "WELL INTEN-TIONED" FARMER	*Narrator:* /// (3 seconds) PERHAPS THAT CAN BEST BE ANSWERED BY A STORY I HEARD MANY YEARS AGO // IT MADE SENSE TO ME AND IT MAY HELP EXPLAIN THE REASON TO YOU // THE STORY GOES LIKE THIS.*
8. Farmer and wife in front of fireplace.	A FARMER TOLD HIS WIFE / "I'LL PLOW THE SOUTH 40 TOMORROW."*

*Cue tones.

Suggestions for Producing Audio Tapes

Producing master tapes. When arranging for production of an audio tape master, provide the following information to the production personnel:

- Type of master and speed at which it is to be produced. (When possible, all masters should be produced on high-quality open reel tape at a speed of *at least* 7½ ips.)
- Number of channels to be used. (When producing audio tapes with cue tones for visual displays, the master should be made in a two-channel format. The voice is recorded on Channel A, and cue signals on Channel B. This provides flexibility in reproduction and editing.)
- Frequency of cue signals to be used. (Although there are currently several standard inaudible cue signals used to control hardware devices, the AV equipment industry is tending toward acceptance of NAVA standards of: 1kHz advance and 150 Hz for stop signals.)
- List of music and sound effects required. (Avoid using home recorded or pirated music. Select music and sound effects from a studio library or purchase stock resources cleared for use.)
- Number and types of talent voices to be used (male and female) and arrangements to be made for hiring professional talent.
- Date master must be completed. (Leave sufficient lead time for final editing and checking.)
- Number of copies of script to be supplied to the production personnel. (Allow one copy each for the sound recording technician, engineer, voice talent(s), the director, and for filing for future reference.)

Ordering Duplicate Copies for Release of Audio Programs

Be sure to order a high-quality duplicate (protection) copy to be made before any work is done.

Specify how many release copies (either reel or cassette) will be required, and the format to be used.

For best results, specify all copies to be made from open reel work copy.

Specify cue tones (if needed) to be audible or inaudible.

Specify the date copies will be needed.

Specify information to be provided on labels.

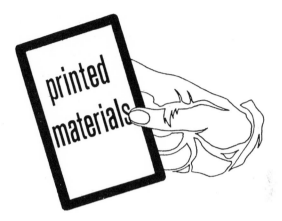

8   Printed Materials

To most of us, the term "printed materials" usually means such professionally produced publications as books, magazines, and manuals. There are, however, a number of other materials that can be called "printed" such as photocopy and offset reproductions, easel sheets, and photographic prints, which often can be produced in-house. These items are widely used in the fields of education and training.

Much discussion has been generated in recent years about the impact of the new electronic media on our society and on its educational and training institutions. There is little doubt that many changes in our thinking and life styles have been a result of electronic media, and other changes surely will continue to appear in the future. However, the impact of the modern media is small in comparison with the changes brought about by the mass distribution of printed material.

In spite of the relatively recent public fascination with new electronic media, it is unlikely that printed materials will ever be eliminated as a vehicle of instruction. It seems equally evident that printed materials will always have an important role in training and education. The trends seem to indicate that in the future, it is likely that printed and other communication media will share responsibilities for supplying content and directions for student learning. Certainly, through the introduction of paperback books and the development of new, rapid, and economical printing processes, people working with training programs have been able to distribute inexpensive textbooks, programmed instruction units, workbooks, and illustrated booklets more conveniently than ever before. Print, in its many forms, can be sent to remote locations and can be used by individuals on a self-instruction basis. The advantages of print seem to expand as technology continues to evolve means of reproducing attractive publications.

Of importance to course developers and writers is recognition of the recent trends in design for instruction and training, as indicated by this quotation from a Ford Foundation report, *An Inquiry Into the Uses of Instructional Technology*, 1973:

> Only within the past two decades have there been serious efforts to evolve a process of textbook development. . . .From these efforts has come the realization that textbooks must be developed in a reiterative process of testing and revision, like programmed instruction and intructional television. And, as in the case of these two other technologies, it has been found that the development of effective textbooks requires a team effort.
>
> Since, for the next few decades at least, the book will continue to be the most widely used instructional technology device, it makes sense to assume it will be possible to make major improvements in the book as a learning tool and to invest extensively in the search for improvements.

When discussing printed media, the subject of programmed instruction inevitably arises, often, unfortunately, because many people think of programmed instruction as "funny little books" that include the student's answers. Although printed material was used during most of the development of programmed instruction, it is, in a broad sense, a set of learning principles and instructional methods that transcend any one medium. The principles of developing clear objectives and appropriate methods of testing and evaluation, the techniques of feedback, reinforcement, prompting, fading, and branching can be applied to instructional design for the use of all types of media. For our purposes here, we will include programmed instruction as a potentially valuable print form that can be incorporated with an instructional program using a variety of media. Again, there are objectives that can be identified for which programmed instruction is the ideal medium for brief, pertinent, and efficiently used instructional units. It is not, however, the scope of this book to attempt a full exploration of this one medium; a few of the many works on programmed instruction are included in the "Selected References" of this book.

Relating Printed Material to Instructional Objectives

Class of media: Instructional medium or instructional aid.

Characteristics: Capable of displaying verbal symbols and still-visual representations, such as artwork, graphics, and photographics.

Application to types of learning:

Cognitive objectives. Printed materials can be used:

To provide factual information such as policies and procedures, or to describe work functions.

To teach recognition and/or discrimination of relevant stimuli.

To present vocabulary used in work functions.

To describe work flow.

To provide a representation of the working location, position, and situations that students will face in the real world.

Psychomotor objectives. Limited application. Although still visuals may be used to teach principles or steps in psychomotor skills and to demonstrate positions of things during motion or the way objects may be held while being manipulated, the display of motion is difficult to represent in this medium.

Affective objectives. Normally does not apply. Although some books are written in a manner that can stir the emotions and can be very interesting, it is unlikely that training materials can be effectively prepared in this manner.

Advantages and Disadvantages of Printed Material

Advantages:

- The student can proceed at his own pace. Lesson material can be designed in a variety of ways to allow for self-paced instruction. This technique can allow for varying learning speeds, dependent on the student's reading ability and entering level skills.
- The student or instructor may easily review the lesson material. The material can also be retained by the student for reference on the job.
- Black and white artwork or photography may be easily adapted to the printed page. When communication problems can be better solved, the cost of two or more color printings may be justified.
- The lesson content is locked in but can be resequenced easily by student or instructor, or by revisions of the materials.
- The lesson materials can be produced economically; distributed easily; updated or revised just as easily; used to display still visuals in either color or black and white; used as either an instructional aid or an instructional medium; and be easily moved from one location to another.

Disadvantages:

- Printing time alone may take from several days to much longer, depending upon the complexity of the material and local services.

- Colored artwork or color photography is usually expensive to adapt to printed material.
- Motion is difficult to show on the printed page.
- Extensive lessons presented in word copy alone tend to turn off and bore students. A similar serious problem can occur with long units of programmed instruction.
- Unless given care, the material can be damaged, lost, or destroyed.

Check List of Considerations for Printed Materials

The following checklist is divided into a series of eight segments listed in sequence. Part A of this list is intended to be used as a mind-jogger to help you review your media selection, while Parts B through H are to help you plan the production of effective lesson materials.

A. REVIEW MEDIA SELECTION. Analyze the proposed lesson content and objectives to determine if this medium is the best one suited to fit your needs. *Unless* the printed material is to be used in combination with another medium, all answers should be answered as indicated in parenthesis.

	YES	NO
Is the material aimed at cognitive learning rather than psychomotor skills or attitude change? (Answer should be YES.)	____	____
Is the display of motion necessary? (Answer should be NO.)	____	____
Is it necessary to present an audio stimulus? (Answer should be NO.)	____	____
Will it be necessary to package and distribute multiple copies of the lesson material? (Answer should be YES.)	____	____

B. ROUGH DRAFT LESSON CONTENT. All answers should be YES.

	YES	NO
Was the rough draft typed in double-spaced copy with substantial margins to facilitate editing?	____	____
Did you use simple words and avoid technical jargon when possible?	____	____
Did you keep the sentences short and directed at the student?	____	____
Did you pencil in areas planned for illustrations or photos?	____	____
Have you planned sufficient area for placing the illustrations or photos so they will be legible?	____	____
Have you noted headings, captions, footnotes, and references where necessary?	____	____
Have you had someone proofread the copy to determine if he understands it? This is also a part of your developmental testing.	____	____
Have you edited to minimize verbal content?	____	____

C. HAVE RETYPED (SINGLE-SPACED) AND RE-EDIT UNTIL SATISFIED.

D. PLAN PAGE LAYOUT AFTER REVIEWING THE MATERIALS ON COMPOSITION AND LAYOUT, following this check list. All answers should be YES.

	YES	NO
Is page layout simple and uncluttered?	_____	_____
Is a consistent format used, being all vertical or all horizontal? (Keep the format consistent so the student doesn't have to turn the book around.)	_____	_____
When using illustrations or photographs to support verbal content, were both formal and informal layouts considered?	_____	_____
Are you planning to use black and white glossy photographs and simple line drawings when possible? (Color photographs adapted to print and artwork are very expensive.)	_____	_____
Will you leave at least a 1-inch margin on the top, side, and bottom of the paper and at least a $1\frac{1}{4}$-inch margin on the side to be holepunched or bound?	_____	_____

E. TEST AND REVISE THE MATERIAL UNTIL ACCEPTABLE FOR FINAL COPY. Review "Developmental Testing."

F. PREPARE FOR PRINTING THE FINAL COPY. All answers should be YES.

	YES	NO
Have you avoided using multiple colors when possible?	_____	_____
Have you considered what design and size of type will be used in the final product and how they can help convey your message?	_____	_____
Have you avoided using a format with a justified (aligned) right-hand margin unless necessary?	_____	_____
Are words to be EMPHASIZED underlined or highlighted in boldface type? (Do *not* overemphasize, or you will lose impact.)	_____	_____
Is the verbal message checked for accuracy of spelling and grammar?	_____	_____
Have you avoided cluttering the typed copy with illustrations? (Leave white space.)	_____	_____
Is there enough space between lines to make the text easy to read? (Be careful not to spread the lines out too much and get a washed out or gray-looking page.)	_____	_____

Is the message to be printed on both sides of the page when possible? (Printing both sides may reduce cost and save paper.)   ____   ____

If necessary, has a proprietary statement been placed at the beginning of the text?   ____   ____

If needed, have you prepared a title sheet?   ____   ____

Are the page numbers correct?   ____   ____

Are the headings and captions accurate?   ____   ____

Is the final copy clean and neat with good black illustrations and clear photographs?   ____   ____

Is the material organized and collated into its proper order?   ____   ____

Do the title sizes complement the text print? (Have you avoided TOO BOLD TITLES that overpower text material?)   ____   ____

G.   ORDER PRINTING AND MATERIALS. All answers should be YES.

YES   NO

Have you considered the weight of the paper stock needed before ordering? (For example, 20-lb. bond stock may be satisfactory for most materials. However, programmed text material may require 60-lb. bond stock to prevent answers from bleeding through.   ____   ____

If necessary, are tab sizes considered? (Tab sheets should be ¼ inch wider than text sheets.)   ____   ____

Has color of paper been considered? (Colored paper for text material is available when there is a reason to use it. Black ink on white or soft green paper gives comfortable readability.)   ____   ____

If material will be updated periodically, has a looseleaf binder been considered?   ____   ____

If hole-punched paper will be used, has the number of holes been determined?   ____   ____

Has type of binder been considered? (If ringed binders will be used, order standard sizes if possible. Unusual sizes cost more.)   ____   ____

Has the required capacity of the binder been determined? (A ½-inch ring binder holds about 40 pages comfortably, a 1-inch, about 80 pages.)   ____   ____

Have the cover and spine design been determined? (Remember, color, unless necessary, may add to the cost.)   ____   ____

Has a logo, trademark, or other necessary identification been designated for the cover?   ____   ____

Has the number of copies for distribution, record files, and replacement been determined?   ____   ____

Have printing cost estimates and promised delivery dates been established? (Always allow sufficient lead time for printing and for reprinting, if necessary.)   ____   ____

H.   PROOF MATERIALS BEFORE DISTRIBUTION.

Suggestions for Page Layout or Composition

In recent years, educators have become increasingly aware of the importance of organization and display in printed materials, in order to maintain student interest and to attract student attention to information. Evidence of this awareness is reflected in the wide variety of book and pamphlet designs currently being published.

Many educational or training materials tend to look like the accompanying sketches.

This layout can sometimes present problems when using illustrations or photographs, or when trying to hold students' attention. When planning a layout, develop *unity* by thinking of the lesson as an entire unit rather than page by page, keeping in mind the following items:

Variety. Printed materials don't *have* to look like the above examples. Sometimes the students' attention can be maintained by varying the layout or by using photographs or cartoons. Also, remember that facing pages make a total display, which can enhance or detract from the effect. At times, facing pages can function as one wide display.

Balance. This too can be used to draw attention or break monotony.

Formal balance is identified by an imaginary axis drawn through the center of the page. This results in a "mirror image" so that one side of the page looks like the other.

Formal *Informal*

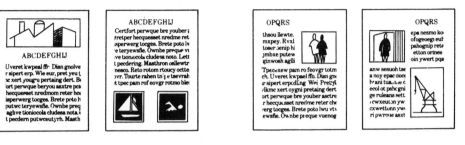

Simplicity. This is another key to good layout design. To achieve it:

Use clean, clear type copy of even, dark intensity.

Use clean, clear, and sharp photographic prints. (black and white glossies if possible).

Use simple, one-color ink drawings if necessary. If possible, don't rely on original artwork. Noncopyrighted clip art can often be used for satisfactory displays, and it is inexpensive.

DO NOT:

Clutter or crowd type copy or illustrations. Leave white space.

Mix type faces except for emphasis.

Make titles so bold that they overpower the text content.

PHYSICAL
OBJECTS
real
things

9 Physical Objects—Real Things

For optimum results from training programs, one widely recommended suggestion is to have learning take place in an environment that approximates actual working conditions as closely as possible. This technique of allowing students to learn tasks in a highly simulated condition generally minimizes the need for students to transfer learning from one environment to another.

Either actual objects or highly simulated mock-ups provide an important stimulus for students to learn tasks that require psychomotor skills. This form of instruction can utilize all of the student's senses, particularly the tactile sense, when learning requires the manipulation of, or interaction with, mechanical devices.

The decision to use real things or simulations depends on a number of working conditions, such as: the safety of students and others, the possibility of damage to expensive equipment, the noise level of the environment, availability of space to conduct instruction, and the cost of supplying expensive equipment for the training activity. There are no simple rules concerning the decision to provide real things or simulations, and each situation must be analyzed separately. For example, the cost of providing simulated flight trainers for airline pilots is great, but when many pilots are trained or given refresher experiences, the cost of simulators is many times less than the costs of using aircraft in actual flight, and the hazards are reduced. However, there are situations in which expensive, hands-on-training equipment is used only because the course was not first submitted to developmental testing to determine if the cost of using actual objects or expensive simulators is actually justified. Each case requires analysis, and often experimental trials. The right tool for the right job seems to be a key thought; how would you feel being a passenger with a novice pilot trained only with a sound–slide presentation?

Since, it is not always feasible to provide instruction in a real working environment or even with the actual objects or devices that students will be coping with on their jobs, frequently compromises must be made. This is necessary to provide safe, effective, and economical instruction and yet imitate actual working conditions as closely as possible. The three most commonly used training techniques for using physical objects are discussed below.

On-Job Training. In this situation learners are able to work with the actual objects of the job within the real work environment.

Hands-On Training. In this situation students still work with the actual tools, devices, machinery, and materials of the job, but not in the actual working environment. This is generally accomplished by bringing the tools, devices, and materials of the job to the student in a classroom.

Simulation Training. The students must work with mock-ups of the actual devices, tools, machinery or other materials from the real world in an environment that simulates the real working situation; performance is similar to that of the real world.

Unfortunately it is impossible to anticipate all the various conditions that might confront the course developer planning to use on-job, hands-on, or even simulations (mock-ups) for training. Each instructional situation will be different and must be evaluated on its own peculiar set of learning requirements, logistics, and job environment. Even the use of different mock-ups will depend on the availability of commercially produced materials or the skills of individual production groups.

Relating Physical Objects to Instructional Objectives

Class of media: Instructional aid and instructional medium.

Characteristics: Can present audio, visual, and tactile stimuli.

Application to types of learning:

Cognitive objectives. These kinds of training can be used to teach recognition and/or discrimination of relevant stimuli. Some examples are:

To demonstrate the sound and appearance of a machine, or other equipment with which the student will be working, or to aid the student to discriminate among sounds and visual cues that indicate malfunctions.

To demonstrate proper and improper methods or techniques used in manipulating tools, equipment, and materials.

The training can also teach rules, principles, or sequential steps in the operation of various tools and equipment.

Psychomotor objectives. These methods are useful for providing student practice or for testing student performance in manipulating tools, pieces of equipment, devices, and materials of the job. They can be used, too, to demonstrate and measure student performance when in the actual work environment.

Affective objectives. When using actual tools or equipment from the job, the probability is increased that students can develop a positive attitude toward their work early in the training period. Attitudes can be positively reinforced by recognizing that their skills develop along with the instruction and the students apprehension about leaving the classroom environment to face real working situations can be reduced.

Advantages and Disadvantages of Using Real Things for Instruction

Advantages:

- Can provide students with maximum amount of realistic job or task simulation, reducing the necessity for transfer of learning.
- Can display all or most of the relevant stimuli from the work environment, yet often with markedly reduced cost.
- Allow students to experience and practice manipulative skills using their tactile sense.
- Permit easy measuring of student performance when physical dexterity or coordination skills are required for job tasks.

Disadvantages:

- Frequently can present safety hazards to students or others in the work environment.

- Can be expensive due to the cost of the equipment and possible damage to it.
- Cannot always present all necessary views of actual objects, such as enlargements, cut-away, and sectioned views; the lesson content must then be supported by other media as required.
- Often it is difficult to find or to hire subject matter experts to conduct on-job training; taking skilled personnel off their jobs to train can reduce productivity.
- It can be difficult to control learning due to conflicts with job or classroom environment.

Check List of Considerations for Selecting and Using Real Things for Instruction

Although using actual tools, devices, equipment, and other materials from the real world can provide many advantages to the learning process, a great number of constraints such as safety, availability of materials, and expense must be imposed on the selection of this medium. Because of the many unique conditions that can be encountered by course developers contemplating the use of this medium, the following check list is abbreviated to only two segments. Part A is to assist in the selection process and presents only the most *critical* decisions that should apply to the selection of physical objects or simulators. The selection process is also divided into three separate parts in order to deal with each form of instruction—on-job training, hands-on training, and simulation or mock-ups—separately.

Because of the many differences in local production facilities, and availability of local commercial suppliers, Part B will simply present some critical suggestions that should apply to the developmental process.

A. Review the decision to use physical objects as a part of the lesson material. *ON-JOB-TRAINING:* All answers should be YES.

	YES	NO
Will the student (and others) be safe working in the real environment with the actual tools or equipment?	____	____
Will the environment be conducive to learning (for example, are the levels of noise and traffic low enough to allow learning to take place efficiently?; will the trainer be able to maintain control over student performance?)	____	____
Will it be economical to use on-job training?	____	____
Is it possible or at least difficult for the student to damage expensive equipment or severely hurt customer relations?	____	____
Will repair or replacement of equipment be inexpensive?	____	____
Will the student become productive sooner by on-job training than by another method?	____	____
Will the work group's productivity and quality of work maintain an acceptable level?	____	____
Are there subject matter experts available and capable to train new students?	____	____

HANDS-ON TRAINING: All answers should be YES.

	YES	*NO*
Will the student (and others) be safe working with the tools or equipment?	____	____
Will the purchase of additional equipment or tools be economically sound?	____	____
Will the classroom environment be conducive to learning?	____	____
If demonstrating equipment, will the area be large enough to permit viewing?	____	____
Will the objects demonstrated be large enough to be seen? (It may be necessary to provide an example for each student, or to use TV for image magnification, or to use correlated projected still visuals.)	____	____
Will the noise and traffic levels be low enough to avoid distraction?	____	____
Will there be sufficient tools or equipment available to prevent excessive student idle time?	____	____
Will any expensive equipment or tools be in a secure location to prevent loss?	____	____
Are there qualified trainers available to conduct classes?	____	____
Will students become productive sooner by hands-on training than by another method?	____	____

SIMULATION OR MOCK-UPS: All answers should be YES.

	YES	*NO*
Are the mock-ups designed to allow the students to be safe?	____	____
Can mock-ups be produced and maintained economically?	____	____
Will the classroom environment support learning?	____	____
Will the mock-ups be large enough to be seen by the class? (It may be necessary to provide a separate mock-up for each student or to use projected visuals for image clarity.)	____	____
Can a mock-up present the students with the necessary stimuli? (Will sound as well as visual and tactile cues be needed?)	____	____
Will there be sufficient material available to prevent excessive student idle time?	____	____
Will students become productive sooner using mock-ups rather than another method of instruction?	____	____

B. Start the developmental process. Consider the following items during this process. All answers should be YES.

	YES	NO
Did you plan to provide proper safety equipment for the students while in class or on the job?	————	————
Will you check the training equipment before class starts to be sure it's in proper working order?	————	————
If using mock-ups, have you checked for commercially produced items already available?	————	————
If using other media to support lesson content to provide enlargements, sectioned, or cut-away views, have you checked to be sure the necessary equipment and visuals are available?	————	————
Have you notified other workers of the new students' starting date, if real equipment and the real environment will be used during the instruction?	————	————

10 Computers

Computers are relatively new as learning tools; they are usually used as a medium for self-instruction or for simulation. Recent advances in the capabilities of computers to interact rapidly with individual students, store vast amounts of information, and display a broad range of audio and visual stimuli, give them the potential to become widely used and useful instructional devices in the near future.

There are two basic forms of computerized instruction used either independently or in mutually supporting roles. We distinguish these forms of instruction as: CAI, meaning Computer Assisted Instruction, and CMI, meaning Computer Managed Instruction. Although these terms tend to be used somewhat interchangeably at times, they are different.

Speaking broadly, CAI is the use of a computer to interact directly with a student for presenting lesson content and testing student progress. Because of the computer's flexibility and capacity to provide branching instruction, it can assume the guidance role of a patient tutor or instructor, while also providing the student with necessary reference materials, simulated laboratory facilities, or clerical services. Depending on the capabilities of the computer and the terminal used by the student, some of the applications of CAI are to display lesson material, provide drill and practice, reinforce learning, simulate environmental conditions, and display relevant stimuli and administer tests.

CMI uses the computer as an aid for the course developer to identify and measure relevant student characteristics, lesson characteristics, help in the design of diagnostic tests, control student's access to lesson materials, redirect students to alternate course lessons, and provide complete data on the progress of individual students or groups of students.

In spite of the many advancements in CAI and CMI in recent years, the medium is not without its problems. Some of the advancements have placed the technology beyond the average course developer's abilities to utilize its potential fully. This frequently results in computers being used as an expensive electronic page turner to display lesson materials. The proliferation of various makes and models of computer hardware devices has dropped the initial investment cost in this medium, but has also resulted in the development of a multitude of incompatible "languages."

It is the author's opinion that before CAI and CMI will be readily available and really practical for widespread application as an instructional medium, a number of major issues must be resolved:

The roles of the course developer (or author) and programmer must be defined. At present a variety of approaches are being tried, but little has been done to determine the most effective and economical means to produce quality lesson material.

More course developers capable of developing complex, branched, programmed instruction must be available.

Languages used between machines and by various software manufacturers must be standardized and simplified.

Efficient and economical distribution systems capable of reaching large numbers of students at many scattered locations must be established.

The cost of both hardware and software must be reduced.

The marriage of computers to a systems approach to instruction will no doubt make a positive contribution to the process of individualized learning. It will also have an impact on the variety of instructional devices currently being used to present lesson material.

Because of the present limited use of CAI and CMI, and since specialized skills are frequently required for programming these materials, suggestions for developing CAI materials will not be included in this text.

Appendix

CHART 1

MEDIA SELECTION
INFORMATION

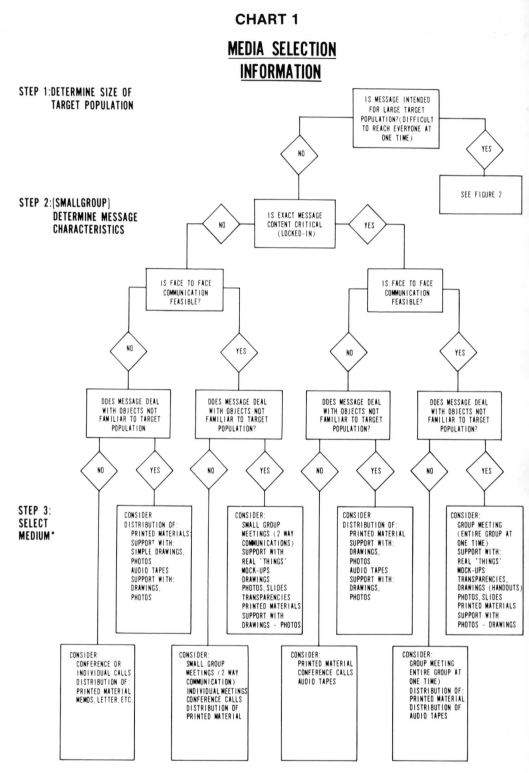

STEP 1: DETERMINE SIZE OF
TARGET POPULATION

IS MESSAGE INTENDED FOR LARGE TARGET POPULATION? (DIFFICULT TO REACH EVERYONE AT ONE TIME)

NO

YES

SEE FIGURE 2

STEP 2: (SMALL GROUP)
DETERMINE MESSAGE
CHARACTERISTICS

IS EXACT MESSAGE CONTENT CRITICAL (LOCKED-IN)

NO

YES

IS FACE TO FACE COMMUNICATION FEASIBLE?

IS FACE TO FACE COMMUNICATION FEASIBLE?

NO   YES

NO   YES

DOES MESSAGE DEAL WITH OBJECTS NOT FAMILIAR TO TARGET POPULATION

DOES MESSAGE DEAL WITH OBJECTS NOT FAMILIAR TO TARGET POPULATION?

DOES MESSAGE DEAL WITH OBJECTS NOT FAMILIAR TO TARGET POPULATION?

DOES MESSAGE DEAL WITH OBJECTS NOT FAMILIAR TO TARGET POPULATION?

NO   YES

NO   YES

NO   YES

NO   YES

STEP 3:
SELECT
MEDIUM*

CONSIDER
DISTRIBUTION OF:
PRINTED MATERIALS:
SUPPORT WITH:
SIMPLE DRAWINGS,
PHOTOS
AUDIO TAPES
SUPPORT WITH:
DRAWINGS,
PHOTOS

CONSIDER:
SMALL GROUP
MEETINGS (2 WAY
COMMUNICATIONS)
SUPPORT WITH
REAL 'THINGS'
MOCK-UPS
DRAWINGS
PHOTOS, SLIDES
TRANSPARENCIES
PRINTED MATERIALS
SUPPORT WITH
DRAWINGS - PHOTOS

CONSIDER
DISTRIBUTION OF:
PRINTED MATERIAL
SUPPORT WITH:
DRAWINGS,
PHOTOS
AUDIO TAPES
SUPPORT WITH:
DRAWINGS,
PHOTOS

CONSIDER:
GROUP MEETING
(ENTIRE GROUP AT
ONE TIME)
SUPPORT WITH:
REAL 'THINGS'
MOCK-UPS
TRANSPARENCIES,
DRAWINGS (HANDOUTS)
PHOTOS, SLIDES
PRINTED MATERIALS
SUPPORT WITH
PHOTOS - DRAWINGS

CONSIDER:
CONFERENCE OR
INDIVIDUAL CALLS
DISTRIBUTION OF:
PRINTED MATERIAL
MEMOS, LETTER, ETC.

CONSIDER:
SMALL GROUP
MEETINGS (2 WAY
COMMUNICATION)
INDIVIDUAL MEETINGS
CONFERENCE CALLS
DISTRIBUTION OF
PRINTED MATERIAL

CONSIDER:
PRINTED MATERIAL
CONFERENCE CALLS
AUDIO TAPES

CONSIDER:
GROUP MEETING
ENTIRE GROUP AT
ONE TIME)
DISTRIBUTION OF:
PRINTED MATERIAL
DISTRIBUTION OF
AUDIO TAPES

* INDIVIDUAL MEDIA LISTED IN SUGGESTED ORDER OF PRIORITY.

CHART 2

MEDIA SELECTION
INFORMATION

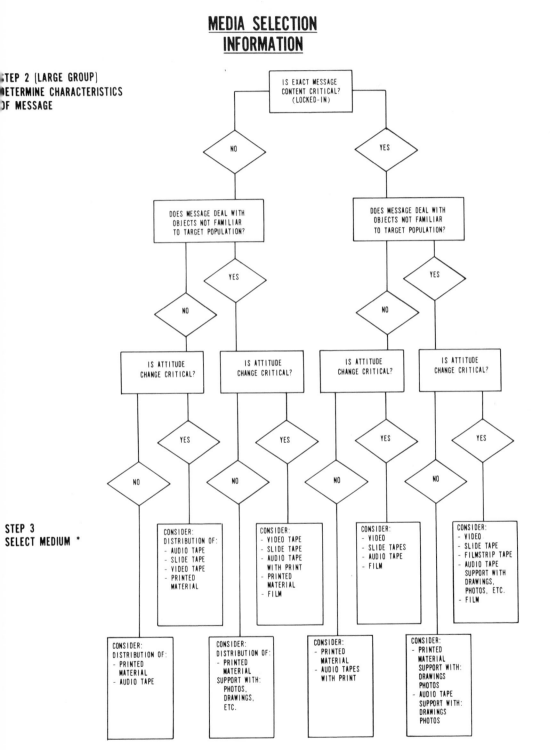

STEP 2 (LARGE GROUP)
DETERMINE CHARACTERISTICS
OF MESSAGE

IS EXACT MESSAGE
CONTENT CRITICAL?
(LOCKED-IN)

NO

YES

DOES MESSAGE DEAL WITH
OBJECTS NOT FAMILIAR
TO TARGET POPULATION?

DOES MESSAGE DEAL WITH
OBJECTS NOT FAMILIAR
TO TARGET POPULATION?

YES

YES

NO

NO

IS ATTITUDE
CHANGE CRITICAL?

IS ATTITUDE
CHANGE CRITICAL?

IS ATTITUDE
CHANGE CRITICAL?

IS ATTITUDE
CHANGE CRITICAL?

YES

YES

YES

YES

NO

NO

NO

NO

STEP 3
SELECT MEDIUM *

CONSIDER:
DISTRIBUTION OF:
- AUDIO TAPE
- SLIDE TAPE
- VIDEO TAPE
- PRINTED
  MATERIAL

CONSIDER:
- VIDEO TAPE
- SLIDE TAPE
- AUDIO TAPE
  WITH PRINT
- PRINTED
  MATERIAL
- FILM

CONSIDER:
- VIDEO
- SLIDE TAPES
- AUDIO TAPE
- FILM

CONSIDER:
- VIDEO
- SLIDE TAPE
- FILMSTRIP TAPE
- AUDIO TAPE
  SUPPORT WITH
  DRAWINGS,
  PHOTOS, ETC.
- FILM

CONSIDER:
DISTRIBUTION OF:
- PRINTED
  MATERIAL
- AUDIO TAPE

CONSIDER:
DISTRIBUTION OF:
- PRINTED
  MATERIAL
  SUPPORT WITH:
  PHOTOS,
  DRAWINGS,
  ETC.

CONSIDER:
- PRINTED
  MATERIAL
- AUDIO TAPES
  WITH PRINT

CONSIDER:
- PRINTED
  MATERIAL
  SUPPORT WITH:
  DRAWINGS
  PHOTOS
- AUDIO TAPE
  SUPPORT WITH:
  DRAWINGS
  PHOTOS

INDIVIDUAL MEDIA SUGGESTED ORDER OF PRIORITY.

CHART 3

SUGGESTED CLASSROOM SEATING FOR SCREEN LEGIBILITY

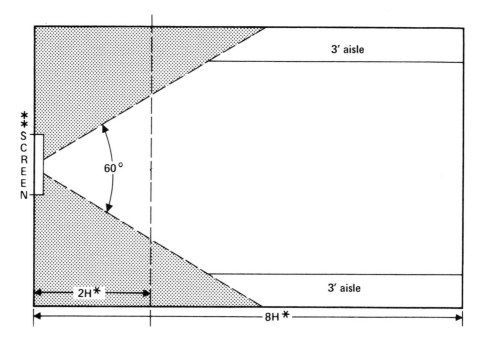

*For maximum legibility, students should be seated within the white area. Students should *not* be seated closer to the screen than two times, nor farther than eight times the *height* of the screen.

**The bottom of the screen should be *at least* four feet above the floor to avoid obstructing the viewing of the students at the back of the room. When a room is arranged for theater style seating, aisles should be placed at the sides and back of the room to maximize viewing area.

A proper sized screen must be provided to ensure 6W legibility standard, one foot of screen *width* must be allowed for each six feet of viewing distance from the screen. For example, a room 25 feet long requires a 50 inch screen, a room 30 feet long requires a 60 inch screen, etc.

(Reprinted by permission of the National Audio-Visual Association, Audio-Visual Equipment Directory.)

CHART 4

LENS FOCAL LENGTH IN RELATION TO:
SCREEN WIDTH AND PROJECTION DISTANCE*

16mm Motion Pictures

Screen Width (inches)

Lens	Proj. Distance (ft)	40	50	60	70	84	96
½"		4.5	5.7	6.7	7.8	9.3	10.6
1"		8.9	11.1	13.3	15.5	18.6	21.2
1½"		13.4	16.7	20.0	23.7	27.9	31.8
2"		17.9	22.3	26.7	31.0	37.2	42.4
2½"		22.3	27.8	33.3	38.8	46.5	53.0

Super 8mm Motion Pictures

Screen Width (inches)

Lens	Proj. Distance (ft)	40	50	60	70	84	96
½"		8.1	10.1	12.0	14.0	16.8	19.2
¾"		12.1	15.1	18.1	21.1	25.2	28.8
1"		16.1	20.1	24.1	28.1	33.7	38.4
1¼"		20.3	25.3	30.4	35.4	42.4	48.4

2" × 2" Double Frame 35mm Slides

Screen Width (inches)

Lens	Proj. Distance (ft)	40	50	60	70	84	96
1"		2.6	3.3	3.9	4.5	5.4	6.1
3"		7.9	9.8	11.6	13.5	16.1	18.3
5"		13.2	16.3	19.4	22.4	26.8	30.5
6"		15.8	19.5	23.2	26.9	32.1	36.6
7"		18.5	22.8	27.1	31.4	37.5	42.7

2" × 2" Super Slides

Screen Width (inches)

Lens	Proj. Distance (ft)	40	50	60	70	84	96
1"		2.4	2.9	3.5	4.1	4.8	5.5
3"		7.2	8.8	10.5	12.2	14.5	16.5
5"		12.0	14.7	17.5	20.3	24.2	27.5
6"		14.4	17.7	21.0	24.3	29.0	33.0
7"		16.7	20.6	24.5	28.4	33.8	38.5

35mm Single Frame Filmstrips

Screen Width (inches)

Lens	Proj. Distance (ft)	40	50	60	70	84	96
3"		11.8	14.6	17.5	20.3	24.2	27.6
4"		15.7	19.5	23.3	27.0	32.3	36.8
5"		19.7	24.4	29.1	33.8	40.4	46.0
6"		23.6	29.3	34.9	40.6	48.5	55.2
7"		27.5	34.1	40.7	47.3	56.5	64.4

Overhead Projection

Screen Width (inches)

Lens	Proj. Distance (ft)	50	60	70	84	96
10.5"		5.5	6.4	7.3	8.6	9.7
12.0"		6.3	7.3	8.4	9.8	11.1
12.5"		6.5	7.6	8.7	10.3	11.6
13.5"		7.0	8.2	9.4	11.1	12.5
15.5"		8.1	9.5	10.8	12.7	14.4

*The lenses listed are selective and do *not* include all the various sizes available. Because of lens manufacturing tolerances, projection distances shown may vary 6" either way. (Reprinted by permission of the National Audio-Visual Association, Audio-Visual Equipment Directory.)

(Reprinted by permission of the National Audio-Visual Association, Audio-Visual Equipment Directory.)

CHART 5

COMMON CASSETTE TAPE FORMATS

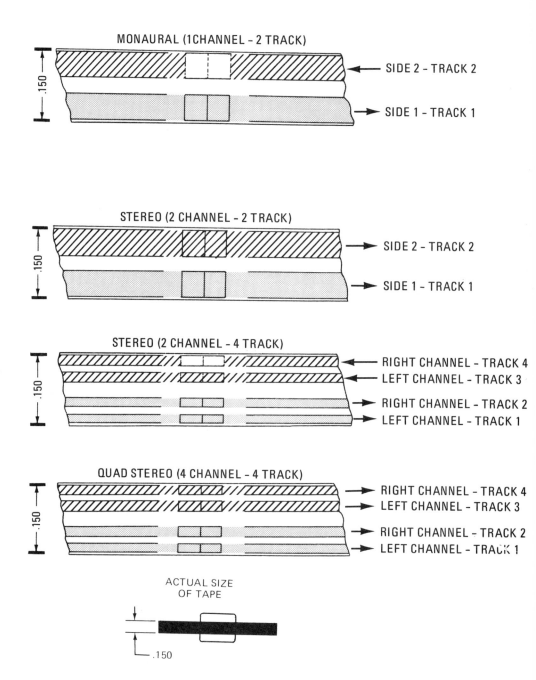

Selected References

A great many resources are available to anyone who wishes to pursue the topics of media, media selection, and instructional development in more depth. The following list represents only a small sample of these sources. The references are categorized somewhat arbitrarily, and they include brief descriptions of content to help readers locate topics of interest. Because some sources are broader in scope than others, they may be listed more than once.

INSTRUCTION—GENERAL

Briggs, Leslie. *Handbook of Procedures for the Design of Instruction.* Pittsburgh: American Institute for Research, 1970. The text presents a set of procedures for the design of instruction, discussing the model as a whole, course objectives, test construction, and media selection. A separate student guide is also available for use with the text.

Brown, J. W., R. B. Lewis, and F. F. Harcleroad. *AV INSTRUCTION: TECHNOLOGY, MEDIA, AND METHODS.* 5th ed. New York: McGraw-Hill Book Company, 1977. Though this is a text directed principally toward using media in formal education at all levels, The principles and background information included can be readily applied to instruction for business, industry, government, and other types of agencies.

Gagne, Robert M. *The Conditions of Learning.* 2nd ed. New York: Holt, Rinehart and Winston, 1970. A discussion of a variety of forms of learning, problem solving, and learning hierarchies. Eight distinguishable classes of performance change (learning) are described, as are corresponding sets of conditions for learning.

Kemp, Jerrold E. *Instructional Design; A Plan for Unit and Course Development.* 2nd ed. Belmont, California: Fearon Publishers, 1976. Suggestions on methods for defining purpose, organizing content, selecting learning methods, and utilizing technological development.

Mager, Robert F. *Developing Attitude Toward Learning.* Belmont, California: Fearon Publishers, 1968. The text deals with the universal instructional objective—how to have students best use and want to know more of what they have been taught.

Mager, Robert F. *Preparing Instructional Objectives.* 2nd ed. Belmont, California: Fearon Publishers, 1975. A self-instructional, programmed text on preparing behavioral objectives.

Popham, W. J., and E. L. Baker. *Establishing Instructional Goals.* Englewood Cliffs, New Jersey: Prentice-Hall, Inc., 1970. A programmed text consisting of self-instructional units dealing with the various aspects of instruction.

INSTRUCTION—PROGRAMMED

Duane, James E., comp. *Individualized Instruction—Programs and Materials: Selected Readings and Bibliography.* Englewood Cliffs, New Jersey: Educational Technology Publications, 1973. A collection of reading and bibliography concerning planning, designing, and implementing individualized instruction programs.

Englewood Cliffs, New Jersey: Educational Technology Publications, 1973. A collection of papers published on individualized instruction from *Educational Technology* magazine.

Hendershot, Carl. *Programmed Learning, A Bibliography of Programs and Presentation Devices.* 4th ed. Bay City, Michigan: 1967, 5th ed. supplement, 1973. An extensive bibliography of programmed instruction materials. A comprehensive list of publishers, systems, devices, and resources.

Markle, Susan M. *Good Frames & Bad: A Grammar of Frame Writing.* 2nd ed. New York: John Wiley & Sons, 1969. An introductory text on the methodology of developing programmed instruction.

Rummler, Geary A., and others. *Managing the Instruction Programming Effort.* Ann Arbor: Bureau of Industrial Relations, University of Michigan, 1967. The text presents aids for assisting industrial organizations to determine if and how programmed learning can solve training problems.

MEDIA AND INSTRUCTION—GENERAL

Armsey, James W., and Norman C. Dahl. *An Inquiry Into The Uses of Instructional Technology.* New York: Ford Foundation, 1973. An examination of the various interpretations of instructional technology, and a review of the current and future use of audio visual media for instruction are presented.

Pipe, Peter. *Practical Programming.* New York: Holt, Rinehart and Winston, 1966. A short, practical book for individuals starting to write programs.

Association for Educational Communications and Technology. Washington D. C. *Selecting Media for Learning: Readings from "Audiovisual Instruction."* 1974. A selected volume of reprints from *Audiovisual Instruction* magazine dealing with selection models, materials, production, marketing, and utilization.

Bretz, Rudy. *A Taxonomy of Communication Media*. Englewood Cliffs, New Jersey: Educational Technology Publications, 1971. The text covers a broad range of communication media and proposes classifications or groupings of various media by their differing capabilities to present stimuli.

Briggs, Leslie J., and others. *Instructional Media; A Procedure for the Design of Multi-Media Instruction; a Critical Review of Research and Suggestions for Future Research*. Pittsburgh: American Institute for Research, 1967. A comprehensive, analytical method of selecting media for instruction is presented by matching media with instructional objectives.

Haney, John B., and Eldon J. Ullmer. *Educational Media and the Teacher*. Dubuque, Iowa: Wm. C. Brown Co. Publishers, 1970. The text presents a discussion on the current uses of media in the classroom and proposes possible applications of media to learning.

Kemp, Jerrold E. *Planning and Producing Audio Visual Materials*. 3rd ed. New York: Thomas Y. Crowell, 1975. A practical, basic volume for media specialists and training personnel in the procedures and processes for production of the major audiovisual media.

Merril, M. David, and Iwrin R. Goodman. *Selecting Instructional Strategies and Media*. C: National Special Media Institutes, 1971. A description of various forms of learning with proposed teaching strategies and media applications.

The State of Knowledge Pertaining to Selection of Cost-Effective Training Methods and Media. Alexandria, Virginia: HUMRRO Technical Report 73-13, 1973. A report on the research conducted by Human Resources Research Organization to provide the Army with a training manual for selecting the most cost-effective training methods and media for specific training tasks.

MEDIA—SPECIFIC

Craig, James, and Susan M. Meyer. *Designing With Type: A Basic Course in Typography*. New York: Watson-Guptill Publications, 1971. The text presents a course in the process of selecting, designing, and laying out printed materials. The text is designed to apply to a wide range of readers.

Dwyer, Francis M. *A Guide for Improving Visualized Instruction*. State College, Pennsylvania: Learning Services, 1972. The guide deals with the effectiveness of visualized instruction in the light of the type of visualization used, the method by which it is presented, and the educational objectives to be achieved.

Kemp, Jerrold. *Planning and Producing Audio Visual Materials*. 3rd ed. New York: Thomas Y. Crowell, 1975. Techniques are presented for preparing and utilizing a wide range of media materials and equipment.

Levien, Roger E., and others. *The Emerging Technology; Instructional Uses of the Computer in Higher Education*. New York: McGraw-Hill, 1972. A study for the nontechnical reader that examines the use of computers in higher education, the current state of the use of computers in general, and the future prospects of Computer Assisted Instruction.

Minor, Ed, and Harvey R. Frye. *Techniques for Producing Visual Instructional Media.* New York: McGraw-Hill, 1970. Detailed "how to" book for illustrating techniques, including mounting, lettering, coloring, and producing transparencies by several methods.

Quick, John, and Herbert Wolff. Small Studio Video Tape Production. Reading, Massachusetts: Addison-Wesley Publishing, 1972. A discussion of methods for selecting equipment, organizing the layout of a small studio, necessary personnel, and ways to produce video programming.

Rilla, Wolf. *The Writer and the Screen.* New York: William Morrow and Company, 1974. A discussion of the various disciplines necessary, and techniques used, in writing for film and television productions.

Tinker, Miles A. *Legibility of Print.* Ames, Iowa: Iowa State University Press, 1963. A summary of studies conducted on the use of various styles and formats of print and their relative readability.

Index

Other Van Nostrand Reinhold Books of Interest

MODERN THEORY AND METHOD IN GROUP TRAINING
Edited by **William G. Dyer,** 252 pp., 6 x 9

Seventeen leading experts bring you new ideas and approaches in the group training field. Experienced in widely diverse areas, these outstanding authorities—training directors, behavioral scientists, group-process observers, and management and organizational development consultants—provide a fuller understanding of this rapidly growing field. Take advantage of their background and knowledge in designing and conducting your own training programs.

PEOPLE-ORIENTED COMPUTOR SYSTEMS
By **Edward A. Tomeski** and **Harold Lazarus,** 320 pp., illus., 6 x 9

Describing why and how computers have failed people and organizations, this book tells what can be done to make these systems serve human needs more effectively. Differing from the vast majority of computer books which concentrate on technical matters, it emphasizes the humane use of computers—since people are the major barriers to their effective utilization. A wide range of unique innovations is emphasized, including involvement of social scientists in computer projects, and use of motivational theory and job enrichment to improve systems design.

NEW PERSPECTIVES IN JOB ENRICHMENT
Edited by **John R. Maher,** 224 pp., illus., 6 x 9

For the manager who aims to keep his employees satisfied with their work and producing at peak efficiency. Includes case studies from companies both large and small—from such diversified environments as an electronics manufacturing plant and a large New York bank—encompassing a broad range of job areas requiring various levels of skill—and all showing the impact of job design on worker morale and productivity. See the successful results obtained by these concerns in achieving new heights of skill utilization, motivation and performance in all their employees, from janitors and cleaning women to top-level professionals.

THE ENCYCLOPEDIA OF MANAGEMENT, Second Edition
Edited by **Carl Heyel,** 1,182 pp., 135 illus., 7 x 10

Put other managers to work for you! Two hundred of them, today's leaders in business and industry, have joined effort in compiling this edition. These contributing authors recognize the fact that most executives reach positions of responsibility in specialized fields, and have only a general knowledge of activities in other management areas. They bring you methods of leadership and their application in many diversified job functions. They show you what other managers are doing—and why. "High level of authoritativeness. . . recommended for all levels of management."
—Industrial Engineering

VAN NOSTRAND REINHOLD COMPANY
450 West 33rd Street, New York, N.Y. 10001